World War I

An Enthralling Guide from Beginning to End

© **Copyright 2022**

All Rights Reserved. No part of this book may be reproduced in any form without permission in writing from the author. Reviewers may quote brief passages in reviews.

Disclaimer: No part of this publication may be reproduced or transmitted in any form or by any means, mechanical or electronic, including photocopying or recording, or by any information storage and retrieval system, or transmitted by email without permission in writing from the publisher.

While all attempts have been made to verify the information provided in this publication, neither the author nor the publisher assumes any responsibility for errors, omissions or contrary interpretations of the subject matter herein.

This book is for entertainment purposes only. The views expressed are those of the author alone, and should not be taken as expert instruction or commands. The reader is responsible for his or her own actions.

Adherence to all applicable laws and regulations, including international, federal, state and local laws governing professional licensing, business practices, advertising and all other aspects of doing business in the US, Canada, UK or any other jurisdiction is the sole responsibility of the purchaser or reader.

Neither the author nor the publisher assumes any responsibility or liability whatsoever on the behalf of the purchaser or reader of these materials. Any perceived slight of any individual or organization is purely unintentional.

Free limited time bonus

Stop for a moment. We have a free bonus set up for you. The problem is this: we forget 90% of everything that we read after 7 days. Crazy fact, right? Here's the solution: we've created a printable, 1-page pdf summary for this book that you're reading now. All you have to do to get your free pdf summary is to go to the following website: https://livetolearn.lpages.co/enthrallinghistory/

Once you do, it will be intuitive. Enjoy, and thank you!

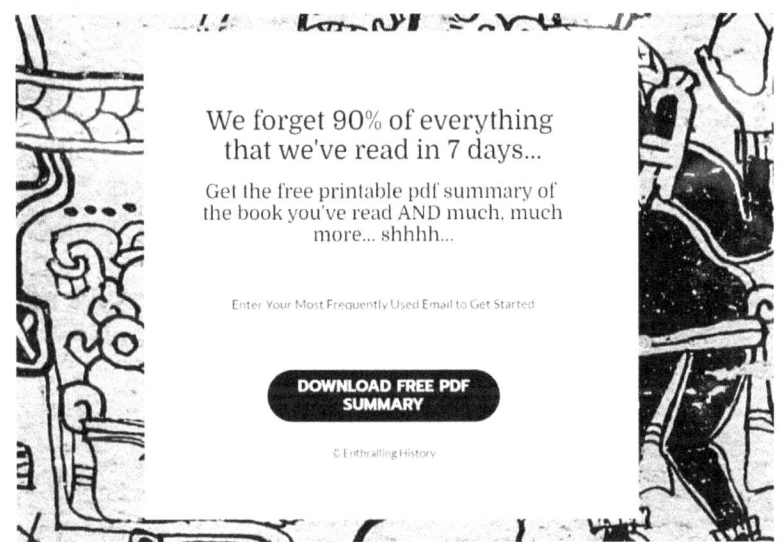

Table of Contents

- INTRODUCTION 1
- PART ONE: UNDERLYING TENSIONS 4
  - CHAPTER ONE – GERMANY VS. FRANCE: ANY EXCUSE FOR REVENGE 5
  - CHAPTER TWO – THE AGE OF INDUSTRIALIZATION AND NEW IMPERIALISM 18
  - CHAPTER THREE – SETTING THE STAGE 33
  - CHAPTER FOUR – ON THE BRINK OF WAR 47
- PART TWO: THE OUTBREAK OF WAR 61
  - CHAPTER FIVE – THE GUNSHOT HEARD AROUND THE WORLD 62
  - CHAPTER SIX – EUROPE AT WAR 78
  - CHAPTER SEVEN – THE START OF THE HOSTILITIES 91
  - CHAPTER EIGHT – THE THEATERS OF WAR 100
- PART THREE – 1915-1916 120
  - CHAPTER NINE – NEW PLAYERS, NEW DEVELOPMENTS 121
  - CHAPTER TEN – THE YEARS OF STALEMATE 139
  - CHAPTER ELEVEN – THE WAR AT SEA 153
  - CHAPTER TWELVE – RUSSIA OUT, UNITED STATES IN 162
- PART FOUR – THE END OF THE WAR 170
  - CHAPTER THIRTEEN – LAST CHANCE FOR GERMANY 171
  - CHAPTER FOURTEEN – THE FALL OF THE CENTRAL POWERS 176
  - CHAPTER FIFTEEN – THE WAR ENDS..................................... 186
- CONCLUSION 196
- HERE'S ANOTHER BOOK BY ENTHRALLING HISTORY THAT YOU MIGHT LIKE 199
- FREE LIMITED TIME BONUS 200
- SOURCES 201

Introduction

The Great War, which lasted from 1914 to 1918, was referred to in Europe as the "war to end all wars." With a total number of casualties ranging anywhere from fourteen to twenty-five million people, history would remember the First World War as one of the deadliest and, at the same time, as one of the most influential wars ever. The four-year conflict was a long time coming for the world, which was rapidly undergoing fundamental transformations in all major areas of life. In fact, because the roots of the war went so deep, lying in historical rivalries and fueled by the desire for revenge, World War I had immense consequences for the international order. The struggle that started in June of 1914 in Serbia quickly spread through all parts of the world due to complex political and cultural ties. These ties were an underlying feature of an increasingly globalized 20th-century world, characterized by the increased importance of power politics and the selfish drive of the European superpowers to assume dominance over their counterparts.

It was this drive that caused the war to escalate to unseen levels, even though Europe had experienced warfare many times before. The war exceeded everyone's expectations; the tight but fragile international order was only one of the factors why the war was referred to as the "one to end all wars." In addition, the technological advancements of the time contributed to this iconic characterization of World War I. The great nations had achieved significant progress in regard to not only civic but also military technology, and the rapid militarization that followed the relatively peaceful period in the late 19th century reached its pinnacle when the war broke out. Thus, by 1914, the world had become increasingly militarized. The nations had grown wary of each other, caused by a multitude of complicated factors that will be explored throughout the course of this book.

Ironically, the First World War only became "the First" after the events of the 1940s, which saw the world descend into chaos yet again. The First World War did not "end all wars" like many, including the winners, had predicted it would. What emerged from the remnants of cities was an even more intricate global system, where the winners of the war enjoyed various privileges while the losers were purposefully isolated and made to feel guilt for the troubles they had caused. The victorious nations tried to implement changes that would ensure peace and stability, but as time would tell, their efforts were all in vain. The international order that was established immediately after World War I would barely last for thirty years. Their attempts failed miserably, and the quick disintegration into yet another world war in 1939 made everyone realize that the model adopted after 1918 was fundamentally flawed. It was based on the redistribution of power at the expense of millions of people who lived in the nations that lost the war. The hardships that were endured by the losers were effectively exploited by the winners, but no one thought that their actions would produce yet another conflict, one that would dwarf the First World War in almost every aspect.

This book seeks to explore the Great War from beginning to end by providing a chronological account of the relevant events that influenced the conflict. In the first part, we will take a look at what exactly caused the war to begin, diving deep into the heightened emotional and political tensions between countries. We will describe the history behind the distribution of power in Europe, as well as the arms race that preceded the Great War, which resulted in its rapid escalation.

Next, the book will cover the actual outbreak of armed warfare, providing a general overview of what the war looked like from the two opposing sides and what the stakes were. We will discuss and analyze the key events and the general characteristics of the first part of the war. Then, the book will focus more on the conflict's military developments by reviewing in-depth accounts of the most important battles that took place, reaching the bloody turning point of the war about two years after its beginning, and the pivotal occurrences that determined the final outcome. Finally, the book will take a look at the last year of the war and assess its conclusion and impact. The events that led to and followed the Paris Peace Conference are vital in truly grasping the long-lasting effects the Great War had on the world.

Part One: Underlying Tensions

Chapter One – Germany vs. France: Any Excuse for Revenge

This chapter will explore the power dynamics established in continental Europe in the later part of the "long nineteenth century," a period of immense importance stretching from the French Revolution until the start of the Great War. The events that occurred during this time are so intertwined that it is impossible to truly speak about them as separate entities, as they all influenced each other in different ways. From the end of the Napoleonic Wars through the unification of Italy and Germany, the developments that took place are pivotal in understanding the roots of the Great War. This chapter will touch upon those events and then focus on the rivalry that developed between France and Germany and the precarious position both sides saw themselves in before the start of the conflict.

The Long Nineteenth Century

The period from the French Revolution of 1789 to the start of World War I in 1914 has come to be known among historians as the "long nineteenth century." This is because the French Revolution is thought to have started a massive shift in the way Europeans looked at politics. The French Revolution saw the French monarchy get overthrown by the people due to it increasingly ignoring the needs and rights of the majority of the population in favor of the nobility and the clergy. The movement that started in France quickly spread throughout Europe, eventually leading to the birth of nationalism, which became a driving factor in the formation of many European states during the 19th century. As a result, more and more European nations started forming their own defined identities and establishing strong nation-states.

Most importantly, following Napoleon Bonaparte's defeat in the 1810s, the Congress of Vienna determined what was next for the future of Europe. In 1815, the Congress of Vienna reorganized the power dynamics of Europe and drew new borders after Napoleon's military endeavors. The negotiations, led by representatives from the four "Great Powers," Russia, Britain, Austria, and Prussia, were perhaps Europe's first real effort at achieving long-term peace and stability in the continent. France was stripped of its recent territorial gains, going back to the borders before Napoleon, and multiple new states were officially recognized in its place. Mainly, the German Confederation was established, which was an entity that incorporated several German territories, including parts of Prussia and Austria. Italy was also divided, with Sicily, Piedmont, and the Papal States, among other Italian factions, emerging as the most important in the region.

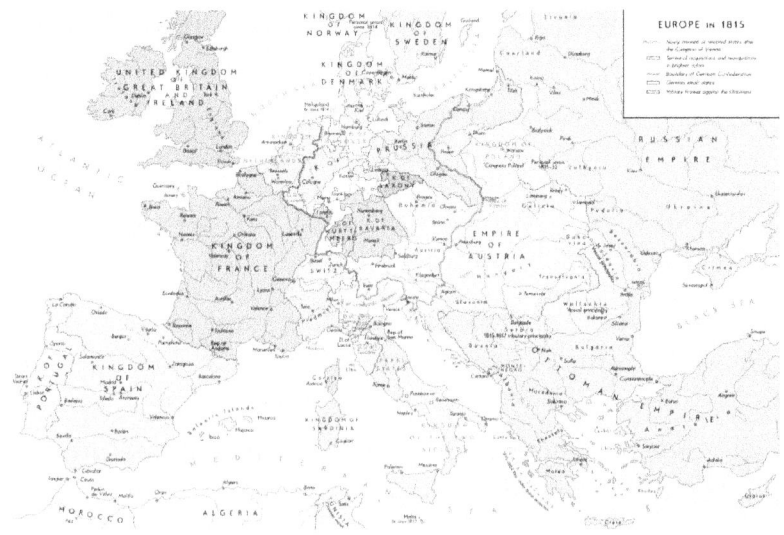

Europe in 1815.

Alexander Altenhof, CC BY-SA 4.0 <https://creativecommons.org/licenses/by-sa/4.0>, via Wikimedia Commons. Accessed from https://commons.wikimedia.org/wiki/File:Europe_1815_map_en.png

An underlying motive behind the Congress of Vienna was the suppression of the revolutionaries, who had become prevalent with the French Revolution and the rise of Napoleon, who had claimed that he wanted to liberate the Europeans from their tyrannical rulers. The Great Powers were all led by conservative monarchies that perceived the rising nationalist voices as a direct threat to their power. Thus, by manipulating the European order, they were able to successfully suppress them, at least for the time being.

The "Old Empires" of Russia and Austria-Hungary were the main advocates of the old regimes and arguably benefited the most from their strengthened position. Britain, on the other hand, was the most stable nation among the Great Powers. It had its house in order, as it enjoyed a balanced system between its parliament and monarchy. Overall, with the Congress of Vienna, the Great Powers managed to divide the continent as they pleased and agreed to pursue stable foreign policies in line with each of their national agendas. They each envisioned different European regions as their own spheres of influence and came to terms for the first time to not interfere with each other's matters.

The Rise of Nationalism and the Unification of Germany

German-speaking Central Europe had always been a strange and complicated political entity. The Holy Roman Empire incorporated the German-speaking peoples of Central Europe, but it was never a stable state because of a multitude of factors, including the sheer number of smaller political units that were under its rule and the unclear chain of command that was in place. As a result, the German provinces largely enjoyed their independence, acting in their own self-interests instead of coming together under a single united German state. Thus, the Holy Roman Empire's position weakened when a province grew more and more powerful because of its individual efforts, challenging the rest for dominance. Other major powers of Europe, like France and Austria, saw their own emergence during much of the late Renaissance. They further reduced Germany's already disjointed political power, as they recognized the threat a united German state could pose in an increasingly competitive Europe.

Thus, one can argue that the German unification process was long overdue and that the preceding events at the beginning of the 19th century were its precursor. Napoleon faced no real difficulties when he took over the disunified, small German states. After his defeat, however, nationalistic ideas became more prominent in all of his conquered territories, including the German Confederation. With the Congress of Vienna, the region saw a period of stability and tried to catch up with the rest of Europe. The Germans realized they were one people, speaking one language and sharing much of the same history, two of the most common factors for forming a nation.

International developments accelerated this process; the period from the 1820s to the 1860s saw massive socio-economic advancements. For instance, Prussia created a German customs union, where all participating states saw positive outcomes, reducing competition among them and paving the way for an even more interconnected road and railway system. The exchange of people and goods took place between the small German states, while Prussia in the north and Austria in the south became two powerhouses that oversaw the political activities in their spheres of influence.

The German dualism that emerged from the clashes of these two rivaling powers decided the course of German unification. One idea was a lesser German solution; in other words, a unification without Austria. The other was the greater Germany option, which included the Austrian-held Holy Roman territories as part of a unified German state. The main problem was that Austria was still largely an absolutist state, and the monarchy was not willing to give up its powerful position. This changed due to developments in Italy that further contributed to the revival of German nationalist sentiment.

In 1859, Piedmont, an Italian state, with the help of France, was able to defeat the Austrian resistance, which had wanted to maintain its influence in northern Italy. This meant Austria's supremacy was dwindling, something that was underlined by the emperor's decision to adopt a new constitution, shifting Austria to a less conservative state.

These events demonstrated that a united effort would yield significant results. What was needed was a leader who would pave the way for consolidating the smaller German states into a larger political entity.

Otto von Bismarck.
https://commons.wikimedia.org/wiki/File:Otto_Von_Bismarck.jpg)

Otto von Bismarck would come to be known in history as the man who created a unified Germany. As the Prussian ambassador to Paris, he was appointed as prime minister by Prussia's Wilhelm (William) I in September of 1862, which was a surprising move to many. The liberal nationalists of the German community, who had advocated for more involvement of the people in governmental decisions, did not like Bismarck. Bismarck was known to have a relatively conservative approach to politics, so the nationalists were not hopeful that he would produce results in line with their views.

Interestingly, however, Bismarck's diplomatic and negotiating skills saw Prussia become increasingly involved in the process of German unification. Whereas the liberal nationalists relied mainly on rhetoric to promote a sense of German nationalism in the people, Bismarck adopted a Realpolitik method, using major developments in Europe to boost support for reunification. His smart, pragmatic approach to international events put Prussia in an increased position of power among its rivals.

With the victory in the Seven Weeks' War with Austria in the summer of 1866, Bismarck was able to significantly weaken Austria's position. He expanded the Prussian realm by annexing several major German territories and formed a new North German Confederation led by Prussia. He made it clear that the process of German unification was underway under the leadership of Berlin rather than Vienna.

German unification concluded some five years later with Bismarck's victory in the Franco-Prussian War (1870–1871). Austria's defeat had signaled grave news for France, which was the other major European power directly affected by the formation of the North German Confederation. A unified Germany meant that the power dynamic would completely shift and challenge French interests. Bismarck knew that Germany was not complete without the southern states joining the union and that the French would most likely oppose him. Thus, both sides were looking forward to an unavoidable conflict, which finally came, thanks to the complex nature of the succession of European monarchies. Prince Leopold of Prussia was considered a candidate for the Spanish throne in 1870, and if he became king, he could further threaten France, which was in danger of being surrounded by members of the Prussian royal family.

In a clever turn of events, Bismarck intercepted and altered the contents of an important diplomatic telegram, manipulating the French into declaring war in July. He motivated the Germans to stand up against the French threat since they were defending themselves. The North German Federation saw multiple victories, one after the other, against the French, eventually leading to the capitulation of Paris in January 1871.

By the time the peace negotiations came to an end in May, Bismarck had already used the patriotic momentum generated by the war to have the southern states agree to join the federation. France also ceded control over the territories of Alsace-Lorraine and was made to pay five billion francs in reparations. With the south German states joining the confederation to form a powerful, united German Empire, Kaiser Wilhelm I was officially proclaimed as the first German emperor in the Palace of Versailles, further adding insult to injury to France. The process of German unification was finally complete.

The Bismarckian Alliance System

The German Reich after 1871.

Deutsches_Reich1.png: kgbergerderivative work: Wiggy!, CC BY-SA 2.5 <https://creativecommons.org/licenses/by-sa/2.5>, via Wikimedia Commons. Accessed from: https://commons.wikimedia.org/wiki/File:Deutsches_Reich_(1871-1918)-en.png

Germany's triumph and France's humiliation did not end with Prussia's victory in 1871. The rivalry that always existed between these two was elevated to an even higher level now that Germany was fully united. In fact, one can argue that by the late 1870s, Germany was the second-most dominant European Great Power after Britain and was rapidly striving to advance in every aspect of life to catch up. The 1870s saw the balance of power that had been established in the Congress of Vienna shift dramatically with the formation of two strong states: Italy and Germany.

Thus, the interests of other powers changed with the rise of these new nations.

Germany had immense economic potential and was industrializing more and more. Its military had become more professional and disciplined; it was on par with the rest of Europe. The opposite was true for Austria-Hungary and France. The Habsburgs started to struggle to keep unity among the many peoples in their vast empire. The different people groups of Austria-Hungary had different fundamental views regarding their political life. It was also becoming apparent that, with the exception of Napoleon's rule, France never really recovered from the revolutionary spirit of the late 18th century, as the sharp differences between the revolutionaries and the loyalists continued to drive a wedge from within.

Since Germany was a newly formed nation that had just been through a couple of wars, Chancellor Bismarck thought that it was logical for Germany to focus more on its internal development rather than divert its attention and resources to external matters. To ensure that the Reich would not be bothered by its neighbors, Bismarck implemented a foreign and security policy that would lay the foundations for the system of alliances that emerged in Europe shortly before the start of World War I. As we have already mentioned, both France and Austria-Hungary were troubled by an array of domestic problems, but the latter was seen as a dwindling empire on the verge of collapse. Although France had also lost a war with Germany, Austria was lacking in economic, social, and military developments.

The Austrian crown had always been hesitant to adopt progressive views when it came to state-building and policymaking since the several different nationalities that comprised the empire were never in tandem. The conservative Austrian Habsburg monarchy was outdated when compared to the ruling systems of other European powers. Plus, due to its lack of cohesion, Austria was not nearly as industrialized, with a major part of the economy being comprised of agriculture. However, despite the somewhat precarious position of Austria-Hungary in the 1870s, Bismarck saw a potential ally since he believed it to be a "European necessity."

Bismarck claimed that he needed Austria-Hungary to separate Germany from the Ottoman Empire and Russia, the latter of which was capable of handling the tension in the Balkans and preventing a war from breaking out in the region. In addition, Bismarck needed to dissuade the Austrians from potentially joining the French in an attempt to seek revenge on Germany. Thus, with all this in mind, he managed to form a *Dreikaiserbund*—the Three Emperors' League—with Austria-Hungary and Russia in 1873 to further isolate France. Struggling Austria was instantly on board, and Russia also accepted, happy to have its roles increased in European politics.

The Three Emperors' League did not continue its existence as a smoothly operating alliance, although it did partially serve its purpose as a balancing mechanism against France. Russia and Austria-Hungary confronted each other after a revolt in the Slavic territories of the Ottoman-controlled Balkans. Russia declared war on the Ottoman Empire, something that was met with fierce resistance from the Austrian crown, which was concerned about Russia's expansionist tendencies. Russia won the war and would have gained significant territorial gains as a result, but Bismarck managed to broker a new agreement at the Berlin

Congress of 1878 between the Austrians and Russians to avoid further escalation of tensions. Thus, the renewed Three Emperors' League existed after 1881, despite Russia and Austria's poor relations. In 1879, Germany entered a mutual military alliance with Austria to demonstrate its firm support and dissuade Russia from potentially starting a war.

If having Austria on its side was not enough to isolate France, the joining of Italy and the formation of the Triple Alliance in 1882 really made it apparent. The Triple Alliance had subtle premises for all its members. Italy was promised help from Germany and Austria-Hungary in the likely event that France declared war—something that the Italians were increasingly wary of after the struggles between the two countries in North Africa. In exchange, Italy was to help Germany in case France attacked and pledged to remain neutral if a war between Austria and Russia broke out. The Austrian troops permanently guarding the Italian border (due to a somewhat hostile history between the two states) could then be freed up to face the Russians on other fronts.

Therefore, shortly after unification, Germany became one of the most active and effective players in European politics. Under Chancellor Otto von Bismarck's leadership, Germany assumed a commanding position in continental Europe with its clever foreign policy, which was aimed at keeping peace in the region so Germany could focus on developing domestically. By the 1880s, what became known as the Bismarckian Alliance System defined the power dynamics between the major European nations. Bismarck knew that Germany was potent enough to endure war with a single nation. Since the main threat was expected to come from the west in the form of revenge-hungry France, he spent a lot of time trying to isolate the French by allying with its rival factions.

Unfortunately, Bismarck's efforts are recognized as a factor in why World War I broke out. The system he organized did ensure peace among the allied nations, but it also promoted competition among those who were left out. As we will see, other European nations soon retaliated and tried to shift the balance of power in their favor.

Chapter Two – The Age of Industrialization and New Imperialism

This chapter will focus on the international factors that are considered to be the precursors to the First World War. Understanding the power dynamics of the involved parties in World War I requires us to examine the states of these actors beyond the borders of the continent.

Pax Britannica

Several major developments took place in the "long nineteenth century" that influenced the political landscape of Europe before World War I broke out. Among them, of course, was the Industrial Revolution, which massively affected the socio-economic structures of European nations. The nation that led industrialization was Great Britain, which was where the Industrial Revolution first took place. Because of this, Britain was given a sort of head start compared to its rivals, causing it to undergo developments of immense magnitude much quicker than its European counterparts for most of the 19th century. Having already established a strong colonial foothold, Britain was able to import goods from its colonies in abundance for cheap and sell it, in turn, for a higher price in an increasingly competitive domestic market. The profits that the British made from colonial trade were huge. And with the technology to process the raw materials into luxury and everyday goods available only to them, Britain quickly became one of the richest nations in the world by the 19th century.

Other factors contributed to Britain's success, such as its convenient geographic location. The British were kept safe from the wars of the tightly packed European nations due to their island locale. This did not limit Britain in asserting its influence in European relations, though. The rise of Napoleon is a clear example. The French emperor was never able to achieve meaningful success against the British, but Britain led the coalition that destroyed Napoleon's ambition to rule all of Europe.

Thus, after the Congress of Vienna, with Europe undergoing a period of stabilization from the Napoleonic Wars, Britain's power grew exponentially to the point that it was the undisputed hegemon of the world in the mid-19th century. This period of British dominance has come to be known as Pax Britannica—the British Peace—whose name was borrowed from the famous Pax Romana of the Roman Empire. Britain's achievements were felt by the whole world. It became an industrial and political powerhouse, fielding a professional army and a world-renown navy and instilling fear among other nations. With peace in Europe, Britain was able to divert its attention to growing and diversifying its domestic market while also extending its reach and becoming a dominant player in the emerging markets of the Middle East, Southeast Asia, Africa, and Latin America. For example, in the first part of the 19th century, Britain signed several agreements with the Arab rulers of the Gulf countries, pledging to protect them from external threats and piracy in return for economic benefits.

Perhaps the most iconic symbol of British dominance is the Royal Navy—something that has persisted as one of the most recognizable characteristics of the nation even today, and rightfully so. At the height of Britain's power, its possessions stretched from North America to Africa to Asia to Oceania. Guaranteeing peace and stability would never have been possible if it wasn't for the constant, effective presence of the British military. The British navy became so advanced and professional because it was the most experienced, having to conduct non-stop operations all around the world since the early colonial days. While other former major colonial powers, such as Spain and Portugal, for example, ceased much of their colonial activity with the turn of the 19th century and continued to lose their overseas possessions in the Americas, Britain largely maintained a firm grip.

The bases for the Royal Navy were scattered all throughout the British colonies, contributing to the formation of a cohesive, effective system and the increase of Britain's overall maritime power. The navy single-handedly controlled the world's trade routes and even provided services other than protection to merchants, such as transportation of expensive, luxury goods that needed to be defended. The unchallenged dominance of the Royal Navy paved the way for Britain's position as a global power and undermined its competitors' advancements for nearly a whole century. It ensured the nation's prosperity by providing protection to the most valuable part of the British economy—colonial and intercontinental trade—as well as to the British Isles in general by dissuading any potential invader from mounting a full-scale assault on British lands.

Resuming Imperialism

With the defeat of Napoleon in the 1810s and the stable period of Europe that followed the Congress of Vienna, what became increasingly clear was the fact that the European territories were not as much up for grabs as they had been before the 19th century. Although wars throughout the continent persevered, it seemed as if the balance of power was finally at a place that was largely acceptable to the European powers, which slowly ceased conducting long-term military campaigns against one another. With some exceptions like the Russo-Ottoman War, Europe in the second half of the 19th century saw no large-scale wars, with the nations instead focusing on internal issues that posed a threat to the political systems in place.

The nationalist movements in Germany and Italy advocated for the formation of a united state. But the conflicts that arose were never on a large, destructive scale, only lasting for short periods of time with low casualties since no side was prepared to contribute adequate resources. Besides, Austria-Hungary and the Ottoman Empires (the "Old Empires") had to deal with multiple rebellions within their borders. Thus, no one really had time to start a war just yet. The European powers became rivals of each other, but the situation never escalated to a large-scale conflict.

Instead, seeing that the options for expansion in continental Europe were limited, the Europeans indulged themselves by contesting each other in the rest of the world.

Colonies were an efficient and reliable source of income, as is apparent from our earlier example of Britain. And now that Europe had been pacified, attention was diverted to challenging each other's interests in different regions of the world. As one could imagine, the technological advancements brought about by the age of industrialization helped the Europeans resume their imperialist intentions after an almost century-long halt. In addition to having access to more sophisticated weaponry, advancements in transportation and communication systems made it easier for the colonizers to better hold onto their colonial gains, which had been a problem in the past. For example, information and goods could be transferred quicker than ever thanks to new railway and telegraph systems, paving the way for a more cohesive approach when trying to increase their foothold in the colonies. Modern medicine also allowed the Europeans to better adapt to the climate and diseases of different geographic locations.

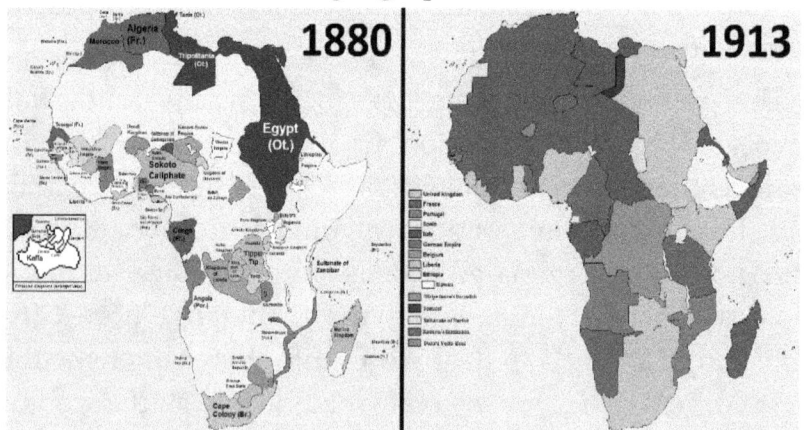

Scramble for Africa.
davidjl123 / Somebody500, CC BY-SA 4.0 <https://creativecommons.org/licenses/by-sa/4.0>, via Wikimedia Commons. Accessed from: https://commons.wikimedia.org/wiki/File:Scramble-for-Africa-1880-1913.png

In the 1880s, after realizing the potential for economic exploitation of the colonies, the European imperialists simply partitioned foreign lands among themselves. During the Berlin Conference of 1884, the continent of Africa was divided by those European powers that had colonial interests. In the Scramble for Africa, as it would come to be known, France, Britain, Germany, Italy, Belgium, Portugal, and Spain drew up new borders of the African continent and came up with several regulations on trade.

As a result, only Ethiopia and Liberia remained sovereign African states, which was quite different from 1880 when only about 10 percent of the continent was effectively colonized. While Britain and France were very much present in the continent before the Berlin Conference, after 1884, the territories under their rule increased in size. Other European states claimed the rest of the continent for themselves. Belgium got the entire basin of the Congo and most of Central Africa; Italy established its colonies in Libya and Somalia; Germany took Namibia and Tanzania; Portugal chose Mozambique in the southeast and Angola in the southwest; France got hold of the island of Madagascar and nearly all of Northwest Africa, including much of the Sahara; and Great Britain's possessions followed the basin of the Nile (including all of Egypt with the recently opened Suez Canal) and included South Africa and parts of West Africa. In short, with the partition of Africa, a new age of imperialism took Europe by storm.

The Europeans vehemently justified their territorial gains in the Age of New Imperialism. They claimed that they brought spiritual and moral enlightenment and material development to the "savage" peoples of the colonies. This feeling of superiority was, in their minds, scientifically proven. In fact, Charles Darwin's newly published thesis, *On the Origin of Species*, perfectly coincided with the Age of New Imperialism. The colonizers used Darwin's scientific findings and manipulated them in a way that benefited their claims. The misinterpretation of complex concepts, like the theories of natural selection and evolution, was one of the reasons behind the Europeans' increased efforts to justify their actions in the colonial world.

Social Darwinism not only applied to the peoples of the world as a whole but also to the Europeans themselves, as different nations perceived one another as more or less culturally advanced. Everyone agreed that Europe stood higher than all other civilizations and that being European was prestigious and beneficial, but the European nations challenged each other for cultural and moral superiority too. For example, the predominantly Orthodox Slavic Europe perceived Russia as their moral, spiritual, and political leader in the clash against Western Catholic Europe. The Germans believed that it was time for the Germanic peoples of Central Europe to reassert their dominance over the Franco-Latins, who had been in power since the days of the Roman Empire. Different statesmen and authors started romanticizing and idealizing this clash of civilizations, coming up with several justifications for why the Europeans should further pursue their efforts of colonization.

All in all, the colonies became a new frontier for the Europeans to challenge each other for regional supremacy. During the latter part of the 19th century, none of the big states were ready to risk war in continental Europe, knowing that a war would only bring destruction to their homes. However, the Europeans never stopped struggling for dominance; they simply moved it to other parts of the world. They were able to subdue much of the colonial world thanks to their technological superiority and the disjointed states of the African, Asian, and Oceanian people. Then, the Europeans justified their actions through pseudoscientific and cultural factors and enjoyed their position as the rulers of the world. The European imperialists significantly grew their power from their colonial gains, something that only contributed to increasing the competition between them. Thus, the renewed imperialist practices and the transformed world order that was established by the end of the 19th century are considered to be indirect but highly influential precursors of World War I.

European Militarism

As Europe became quieter in the 1880s and 1890s, the European powers started investing more in developing better military and weapons systems. The relative peace established after nationalism triumphed in Italy and Germany, in addition to the expansion of Europe's imperialist strength, resulted in the birth of militarism in major European nations. They spent a significant portion of their income on improving their capabilities during wartime. As a result, the final decades leading up to World War I are characterized by a European arms race.

The roots of 19th-century German militarism can be traced back to the years before its unification, right after Napoleon's defeat. When Napoleon defeated the Prussians, King Frederick William III agreed to reduce the Prussian military's size to a mere forty-two thousand active troops. However, the king implemented a smart tactic; he conscripted and trained new troops every year for a one-year period and then dismissed them from service. This meant that even though the Prussian military immediately after the Napoleonic Wars was comprised of 42,000 active men, ten years later, there were 420,000 Prussians who had undergone at least a year of military training and could have been called up if the situation proved dire.

The Prussian military's readiness during the events of the 1860s and 1870s helped the kingdom lead the process of German unification and defeat the Austrians and French without much difficulty. France's rapid defeat in 1871 further supported the fact that Prussia had a more professional force than its neighbors, and a unified Germany under Prussian leadership would expand the army's capabilities even more. Thus, to no one's surprise, the efforts to further modernize and improve the German military continued after the reunification, and the system became well organized, relying on a strict hierarchy with the Kaiser at the top followed by a military council comprised of generals and officers of landowning *Junker* nobility. The German parliament had no say in the military decisions; it could only advise the council and the chief of general on needed occasions and left the military in the hands of the professionals.

Overall, the spending on the German military after unification increased dramatically, almost by 70 percent, reaching about $460 million by 1913. France, Russia, and Italy soon followed, although the sheer industrial power held by the Germans made it difficult for the competition to catch up. It was correctly perceived by the European powers that if a conflict broke out in Europe, the direct clashes of armies on open fields would decide the outcome, thus justifying their decision to increase conscription to have as many men available as necessary.

Technological advancements also played a role. Military industrialists closely observed and studied the conflicts of the 19th century and introduced improvements to weapons systems. Again, the main focus was on improving heavy artillery by, for example, increasing the range of fire without sacrificing too much mobility. New types of explosive shells made their way into the arsenals of European nations, and small and large firearms were developed to be more portable and deadly. New regiments and battalions were created to field these improvements. All in all, the upgraded weapons systems slowly caused a shift in the way the European powers regarded warfare.

The abovementioned developments generally increased the competitiveness of European powers, but militarism managed to touch other parts of the world that would eventually become involved in World War I, namely Japan and the United States. Dominant actors in their own respect, these nations also built up their militaries and exercised similar practices in the decades leading up to 1914, in turn increasing their own positions of power in their respective regions.

From the second half of the 19th century to the start of the First World War, all of the major powers implemented significant reforms to boost the competence of their militaries. One underlying feature was the implementation of action plans in case a war broke out. Quick offensive strategies, which allowed the attacker to rapidly overwhelm the defenders to achieve decisive victories, became prominent. Nearly all of the powers had these plans ready before World War I.

In an interesting turn of events, Germany would find itself in a new rivalry with arguably the strongest power of the world at the time: Great Britain. As we have already mentioned above, the British Royal Navy proved crucial for Britain's international success and enabled it to reach a dominant position as a global hegemon. The navy was virtually unchallenged and the most experienced and advanced. It kept steadily growing in size since Britain's colonial activity never ceased, unlike other European powers in the 19th century.

In addition, after achieving victories in multiple naval battles, it became clear that having a powerful navy was the key to increasing a state's power. However, no state had invested as much as Britain in developing naval capabilities. They all, in a way, accepted Britain's supremacy on the high seas. The Spanish and the French had tried multiple times but suffered losses against the British on different occasions, most famously in the Battle of Trafalgar when a combined Franco-Spanish fleet was crushed by Admiral Horatio Nelson of the Royal Navy. The United States had practiced an isolationist policy for much of its existence and did not wish to challenge Britain on the seas. The disadvantageous geographic location of Russia and Austria-Hungary and their lack of access to the seas meant they had no interest in building up their fleets to compete with the British. Thus, with no competition, Britain continued to dominate.

The situation would change drastically in the 1890s when Germany prioritized building a strong navy. Several factors precipitated this development, the most important of which probably was the publishing of a very influential work about contemporary naval strategy titled *The Influence of Sea Power upon History* by an American naval officer named Alfred Thayer Mahan. Mahan asserted that there was a direct relationship between possessing a strong navy and global supremacy. He stressed that achieving world domination and emerging as powerful actors on the international scene was determined by sea power, and in the seas, whoever had the bigger fleet would usually reign supreme.

Influenced by Mahan's thorough analysis of the global balance of power and naval strategies, Germany diverted its efforts to building a naval force strong enough to pose a threat to the unquestionable British dominance on the seas. Kaiser Wilhelm II put Admiral Alfred von Tirpitz in charge of the navy since both had similar views on the matter. They increasingly lobbied the Reichstag for funding for their projects, leading to the five German Fleet Acts (1898–1912), which saw huge amounts invested in their cause and substantially increased Germany's naval power. Admiral Tirpitz envisioned Germany's fleet to be about two-thirds the size of Britain's so that, in case of war, it would not be possible for the latter to simply bully Germany on the seas.

However, Britain did not just sit back and watch as one of its main European rivals continued gaining power. The passing of the Second German Fleet Act in June 1900 served as a wake-up call for the British, who tried to answer the Germans by increasing their own naval capabilities. British Admiral Jacky Fisher proposed different measures to counter German efforts in 1902. He ordered a large part of the Royal Navy, which had been scattered around the world to patrol the seas, to return to the British homeland so they could mobilize quicker.

The HMS Dreadnought, 1906.

https://commons.wikimedia.org/wiki/File:HMS_Dreadnought_1906_H63596.jpg

In addition, a major development altered the approach of the two powers when it came to their navies. A new super battleship, the HMS *Dreadnought*, was launched. It was equipped with the newest weapons and dwarfed all other warships. Upon its launch in 1906, the HMS *Dreadnought* was the most powerful—wielding the strength of three normal battleships—and the most expensive, with the British having spent upward of about 1.7 million pounds on just the first model. The commissioning of the warship gave birth to a completely new line of warships conveniently nicknamed "dreadnoughts." They modernized sea warfare and were viewed by the world as a necessity to keep up with militarization efforts. By the start of the war, powers around the world had invested in their own dreadnoughts, but it became clear that Germany had put the most effort into catching up with Britain since its funding and number of personnel increased dramatically.

The naval arms race, as it would come to be known, would continue on different levels until 1912. Different international events, like the Russo-Japanese War, would further prove Mahan's points about naval strategy. Beginning in 1912, German Chancellor Theobald von Bethmann Hollweg would prioritize building the army since Germany had achieved its primary objective of becoming a viable power on the seas. The situation in continental Europe was becoming more worrying, so it was practical to focus on building up ground forces. However, Germany also began the development of military submarines, a completely new and revolutionary technology that was kept secret from the rest of the world. Britain, on the other hand, stopped investing in the Royal Navy since it thought that it was still substantially ahead of the competition.

A 1909 cartoon from Puck showcasing the European naval arms race.

https://commons.wikimedia.org/wiki/File:Naval-race-1909.jpg

All in all, competition increased among the European superpowers, despite the fact that their rivalries never escalated to war. Each state prioritized militarization as they grew wary of the quiet international order and expected war. With the influx of new technology as a result of industrialization, they continued their struggle for dominance in the Age of New Imperialism by competing with each other through their colonies. At the turn of the 20th century, it seemed as if the world was ripe for another major war.

Chapter Three – Setting the Stage

There is no doubt that after the age of Napoleon, the world underwent a massive transformation in all areas of life. Nationalist and liberal movements breezed through Europe, leaving their mark on emerging new powers. New players emerged in the new and old worlds as the Europeans sought to partition the colonial lands among themselves. And rivals began rapid military mobilization, cautious of a potential conflict that could break out.

This chapter will explore a major factor behind the quick escalation of World War I: the European alliance system. Shortly before the start of the war, two main alliances emerged that sharply divided the superpowers. Although the initial intent of both alliances was to balance the levels of power and influence as a countermeasure to war, ironically, this complex relationship would drag European states into the First World War not long after it started.

New German Foreign Policy

Chancellor Otto von Bismarck saw France as the main and natural threat to Germany, so the measures discussed in the previous chapters were aimed at preventing France from forming strong connections with other powers and from regaining some of the might the French had lost since the days of Napoleon. The Three Emperors' League served that purpose, and by working with Austria and Russia, Bismarck significantly strengthened Germany's position of Germany while undermining France. The Triple Alliance with Italy and Austria was also conceived to provide an effective response to a potential French offensive on Italian and German positions. The security provided by these treaties put Germany in a comfortable position, allowing it to focus on its internal development and build up its industry and military.

However, German foreign policy significantly changed after Bismarck left office in 1890. Kaiser Wilhelm II saw a different course for Germany, one aimed at increasing its influence and power not only regionally but also globally. This was in fundamental opposition to Bismarck's earlier policies, which were mainly directed at keeping peace in Europe by dissuading nations from going to war with each other and relying on domestic production to gain more wealth. In fact, Wilhelm II's efforts to make Germany a player in the colonial game were arguably based on the country's domestic improvements. Had Germany not achieved immense economic growth in the 1880s, the Kaiser's ambitions of expanding the country's power would have been baseless and illogical. The naval arms race with Britain served the same purpose. Germany was able to continue investing millions in developing its navy because of its strong economy.

Thus, Kaiser Wilhelm II decided not to renew Bismarck's agreement with Russia. According to the Reinsurance Treaty, which had been signed in 1887, both sides would declare neutrality in case of an attack on either France or Austria. The Reinsurance Treaty was a guarantee for Germany that Russia—a European power that had immense military potential due to the sheer size of its army—was not a threat.

After the treaty was dropped in 1890 by Germany, Russia naturally felt betrayed and started seeing its former partner as a potential enemy. This opportunity was used by the French. France and Russia entered into a mutual military alliance, something that was extremely beneficial for both sides since they lacked friends. The new Franco-Russian alliance redistributed the balance of power in Europe, with Germany now sandwiched between two nations that were unfriendly toward it. The alliance was especially crucial for Russia, as it borrowed millions from Paris to finance development projects in industry and infrastructure. These funds were mainly invested in building a trans-Siberian railway, which would connect the European part of Russia with the east. In addition, Russia managed to negotiate with Austria on the Balkan matter, signing an agreement and putting their differences aside for the next ten years. This freed up more of Russia's resources to be used elsewhere, further boosting internal development and raising its capability on the international stage.

Britain in Search of Allies

Additional events transpired that further intertwined the fates of world superpowers. A major development was a new British foreign policy. British concerns arose predominantly in response to the increased industrialization and militarization of the European powers, something that Britain correctly believed would challenge its supremacy as a global hegemon. Despite the fact that the Royal Navy was still the ruler of the high seas, the naval arms race with Germany, as well as the naval reforms of countries like the United States, Japan, and France, meant that the British might not enjoy such a prestigious position for long. For a very long time, Britain's isolation had managed to keep it out of complex foreign affairs and provided the kingdom with the possibility to expand its reach. However, it was becoming apparent that Britain needed friends it could rely on, especially since other states were forming close relations with each other.

Thus, Britain's foreign and security policies in the final years of the 19th century were directed to forge ties with states with which Britain shared interests, especially when it came to colonial matters in Asia—a region that had become of the utmost importance. While Germany was emerging as Britain's direct rival, a series of talks took place between the two sides to reach a mutual understanding regarding several pressing matters. However, between 1898 and 1901, in three different instances, Anglo-German talks broke down, leading to deterioration between the two states.

Britain decided to implement a smarter strategy by increasingly working with nations that were considered German rivals, which served to undermine Germany's progress by preventing it from further extending its global reach. Britain signed the Hay-Pauncefote Treaty with the United States in 1901, reaching an agreement about the terms of building the Panama Canal, which was extremely beneficial for both sides. About a year later, in January 1902,

Britain managed to form an alliance with Japan—a nation that had significantly grown its power after the Meiji Restoration and had established itself as perhaps the most influential actor in East Asia. The relations between the two states were already on somewhat good terms after the signing of a new trade agreement in the mid-1890s, and the alliance was perceived as beneficial for both sides. It undermined Russia's power in the region and allowed Britain to focus more of its resources on India.

Then, in 1904, as Japan and Russia were about to descend into war over Manchuria, Britain realized that its alliance with Japan would potentially drag it into conflict with France, which was an ally of Russia. Thus, to avoid an escalation both in Europe and in the colonies, Britain and France set aside their historical differences and decided to sit together at the negotiation table. In April, the two sides agreed to the Entente Cordiale. This agreement was not an official defensive or military alliance but served to improve the relations between the two nations. The Entente Cordiale was the first real step in forming deep Franco-British ties. It focused on clearing up the colonial disputes of the two sides in previously contested territories, mainly by giving up French claims on British Egypt and by Britain supporting the French occupation of Morocco. Several other points of contention were also cleared up in other parts of the world.

In the big picture, this agreement between France and Britain was, in a way, the end to the international isolation both nations had experienced for much of the 19th century. France regained some of its power through a new ally, while Britain now had amicable relations with the Reich's main rival. As we will see later on, the Entente Cordiale became the foundation for the cooperation between France and

Britain, with both continuing their efforts of deepening diplomatic ties in case of future international crises. All in all, in the span of four years, Britain managed to gain several partners it could rely on, something that served to reassert its position as the biggest global superpower and subdue its challenger, Germany.

The First Moroccan Crisis

The Entente Cordiale did not go unnoticed by Germany, which became wary of the improved relations between its rivals. Despite the fact that Germany had become one of the most economically prosperous nations with a professional military, the developments from 1901 to 1904 only served to reduce its overall influence on the international stage. Germany had not seen any benefits from allying with Austria and Italy since the Triple Alliance's nature was strictly defensive and served to deter a potential French invasion. France and Britain were happy with their increasing presence in their colonies and did not demonstrate an interest in expanding in Europe. What followed the signing of the Entente Cordiale was a provocatory German reaction aimed at undermining the relationship between the French and the British.

It is important to understand that by the time the Entente Cordiale was signed, Morocco was one of the remaining African nations not under the direct rule of a European nation. The French and Spanish had both expressed interest in Morocco during the Berlin Conference, but their approach did not include direct occupation or the use of force. Over time, Morocco became a sphere of influence for both of these nations, with France and Spain seeking economic gains, something that was frowned upon by the Germans due to the increased presence of the French.

When Kaiser Wilhelm II arrived in the Moroccan city of Tangier on March 31st, 1905, he toured the whole city, which had gone into a parade for his presence, on a white horse and declared his support for the Moroccan sultan. The move was seen by Paris as an insult to France. After the Kaiser's speech, Sultan Abdelaziz felt compelled to invite the European powers to advise him on how to reform the country instead of going through with the reforms presented to him by the French prior to the Kaiser's visit. France naturally believed there was no need to hold such a conference, while German Chancellor Bernhard von Bülow threatened to sign an alliance treaty with the sultan if the French presence in Morocco was not discussed with the other nations.

Thus, France was forced to take part in the Algeciras Conference, which took place at the beginning of 1906. Despite this, only one other nation at the conference— Austria—supported Germany. The overwhelming majority, including the US, Russia, and Italy, took France's side. Most importantly, Britain decided to firmly side with France, demonstrating that it was more than ready to pursue the Entente Cordiale. In fact, it is argued that Germany had acted to see how strong Franco-British relations were and undermined the treaty's importance by provoking both nations. France saw success in reorganizing Morocco by increasing its presence through several policies while leaving some power to the sultan. Additionally, France and Spain signed the Pact of Cartagena a year later, officially recognizing each other's spheres of influence and excluding Germany from matters in Morocco. All in all, the First Moroccan Crisis did not diminish the Franco-British relations as Germany had desired. Instead, it made it clear that both Britain and France were willing to challenge

Germany.

The Russo-Japanese War

Along with the First Moroccan Crisis, the Russo-Japanese War was another major international development that contributed to the world alliance systems.

Japan was a rapidly modernizing nation that sought to catch up to the European powers and become an influential actor on the world scene. It had made quite an effort to increase its regional presence since the Meiji Restoration in the mid-19th century. In fact, Japan's imperial ambitions, as well as many of its ideas regarding modernism and development, were influenced by prior European endeavors. After defeating China in the Sino-Japanese War, it became clear that Japan was the strongest independent power in East Asia since the rest of the region was composed of European colonies. None of them were strong enough to challenge Japan except for Britain, but the two sides had agreed to an alliance in 1902 that permitted them to pursue mutual interests—economic gains and rich naval trade routes for Britain and the ability to expand for Japan.

Naturally, the main rival that emerged against Japan's imperialistic intentions was Russia, a nation that had expanded its possessions to include all of northern and northeastern Asia. The founding of the major Pacific port city of Vladivostok (which translates to "the ruler of the East") was the most apparent sign of Russia's ambition to secure its eastern flank and cement itself as a major actor in East Asian politics. The Russians wanted to establish a permanent presence in the Pacific to enable an influx of new trade routes to the country from the east. For that reason, Russia leased the naval base at Port Arthur from the Chinese in 1897. However, both ports were only operational during summertime and froze during winter. Thus, both the Russians and the Japanese eyed Manchuria and Korea.

Japan acted first. It realized that neither Korea nor Manchuria would be able to resist the two countries and offered to divide the territories with Russia. Korea would become part of Japan's sphere of influence, while Russia would be free to pursue its interests in Manchuria. As a counter-offer, Russia wanted to organize a buffer zone between the two sides along the 39th north parallel in Korea, which directly clashed with Japanese ambitions, prompting them to declare war. In a surprise attack, the Japanese engaged with the Russian fleet stationed at Port Arthur in February, striking a heavy blow. The Russian response was swift but not effective. The Russian army lacked discipline and heavily relied on numbers to overwhelm the opposition. But the majority of Russia's forces were not mobilized in the east, and transporting them from western Russia was a long and tenuous process. Even when they came into contact with the Japanese, they suffered multiple defeats since Japan had a more professional, battle-ready core with high morale. In addition to that, Russia's main fleet was also in Europe, and it only managed to get to the Sea of Japan in May 1905, by which time the Japanese had significantly reduced the Russian presence and achieved a decisive victory in the naval Battle of Tsushima.

The war ended with the Treaty of Portsmouth, which was negotiated by US President Theodore Roosevelt. After it became clear that the Japanese were on par with the Russians, anti-war sentiment swept the country. Combined with an array of social and economic problems, it resulted in the 1905 Russian Revolution. Tsar Nicholas II, who fully believed that Russia was capable of defeating Japan, and had hoped to achieve a quick victory to pacify his critics, was forced to agree to difficult terms. Japan got hold of Korea, which it eventually annexed in 1910, while Russia evacuated all of its forces from Manchuria, significantly reducing its strength in East Asia.

More importantly, the Russo-Japanese War proved that Japan was a true superpower and had the ability to challenge and even defeat the Europeans. The Japanese victory made it clear that Britain had made another successful foreign policy move by allying with Japan and had correctly predicted Russia's demise in East Asia. On the other hand, Tsar Nicholas II realized that his prospects of expanding in the Pacific had dwindled. The defeat made him reignite Russian interest in the Balkans.

The Triple Entente

The First Moroccan Crisis and the defeat of Russia in the Russo-Japanese War had repercussions on the European balance of power. In an interesting turn of events, the British alliance with Japan had proven to be a smart move, as Japan established itself as a force to be reckoned with in the Pacific.

Naturally, the nation that did not see any real benefits from the two international events was Germany. German efforts to undermine the Entente Cordiale between France and Britain were ineffective. In fact, its efforts in Morocco had the complete opposite effect, strengthening the ties between the two nations. Germany only found support from the Austrians during the Algeciras Conference. Even Italy, which supposedly had friendly relations with both Germany and Austria, backed French interests in Morocco in exchange for French support in Libya.

The Russo-Japanese War showed that the Russian army, despite its size and former glory, still needed to undergo massive changes to modernize, thus undermining the severity of the Russian threat to Germany. However, France was more than happy to provide funds to Russia to rebuild and play catch up. In short, after Bismarck left office in 1890, with the exception of the Berlin Conference, nothing had really played out in favor of the Reich. The arms race with Britain had prompted it to abandon isolation, causing Germany's main threats to come together to unite against the rising German nation.

The troubles for Germany did not end there, as Britain, France, and Russia continued to engage with each other in new diplomatic talks. Tsar Nicholas II was desperate to consolidate his internal power. Faced with instability and revolution back home, he was ready to give up much of Russia's imperial interests in exchange for much-needed economic support. Thus, in another shocking foreign policy move, Britain decided to backtrack from its not-so-positive relations with St. Petersburg and initiate the Anglo-Russian Convention of 1907. The two sides agreed to terms regarding their interests in Afghanistan and Persia. Britain was heavily dependent on imports from the Indian subcontinent. Since the territories in contention directly bordered India, it was happy to clear up the disputes it had with Russia, which considered Persia and Afghanistan as its own sphere of influence. As in the case of the Entente Cordiale with France, Britain was willing to put an end to its old rivalry for the sake of pursuing mutual interests that indirectly contributed to Germany's further deterioration.

It made sense that the bilateral agreements between Britain and France, France and Russia, and Britain and

Russia finally led to the creation of the most important World War I alliance—the Triple Entente. Although the Triple Entente was not a mutually defensive alliance (meaning that in the case of an attack on one member, the other two did not have to necessarily interfere), it clearly underlined that cooperation existed between the three countries. It was more of a coalition, similar to what the European powers had done during Napoleon's reign. It served as a balancing mechanism against the German-Austrian axis and emerged as a direct rival to the Triple Alliance between Austria, Germany, and Italy.

France and Britain continued their efforts of clearing up colonial disputes while also sending economic aid to Russia to speed up its development and help St. Petersburg overcome the effects of the revolution. In addition, they mediated better relations between the Japanese and Russians to avoid another potential conflict in East Asia, which likely would have been more destructive. Paris concluded an agreement with Tokyo in 1907 that tied the two nations closer together and played a big part in stabilizing the relations between Japan and Russia. Putting the war behind, Japan willingly accepted France's proposal and no longer perceived Russia as a threat to its interests in East Asia, something that was also partly due to the close relations between Moscow and Paris.

European Alliance Systems by 1914.

Historicair (French original) Fluteflute & User: Bibi Saint-Pol (English translation), CC BY-SA 2.5 <https://creativecommons.org/licenses/by-sa/2.5>, via Wikimedia Commons. Accessed from: https://commons.wikimedia.org/wiki/File:Map_Europe_alliances_1914-en.svg

Thus, in the first ten years of the 20th century, the international order saw yet another fundamental transformation. The German efforts to abandon Bismarck's foreign policy of keeping peace in Europe by isolating their direct rivals in favor of pursuing a more prominent *Weltpolitik* did not prove to be a smart decision. Challenging Britain for international dominance in the naval arms race was becoming more and more costly for Berlin, and the active role that the Reich assumed did not go unnoticed by Germany's rivals. Britain realized that it was impossible to keep its vast empire without international partners and started to slowly forge relations with different actors to obtain a firmer grip on its colonial possessions, which were the main source of its income and prestige. Britain's alliance with Japan, agreements with the United States, and ententes with Russia and France served the British government well.

The Triple Entente was an immensely beneficial agreement for France as well. It tried to retaliate against

Germany, which had pursued a policy of isolating France since the early 1880s. By forming close relations with Britain, Russia, and Japan, France was given a much-needed way back into becoming one of the biggest players in world politics. In addition, the Triple Entente could be helpful against a potential German threat. Russia, unlike the other powers, just sought to buy time and solve an array of problems, such as the revolution and the war with Japan. It was becoming evident that the next major European conflict would have massive repercussions for the whole world.

Chapter Four – On the Brink of War

The emerging alliance systems were a byproduct of new powerful international actors that had risen into prominence in the later part of the 19th century. Britain recognized that Germany's rise might challenge its global hegemony and decided to forge connections with nations to govern its vast colonial possessions and potentially deter the Germans from catching up. Germany, on the other hand, abandoned the Bismarckian alliance system that was primarily aimed at keeping peace in Europe. Instead, it shifted its focus to world domination, something that proved to be costly since its rivals soon realized the threat Germany posed and balanced it out with their own efforts.

This chapter will explore the final pieces of the puzzle of what led to World War I. We will take a look at the old-fashioned structures of the European empires, as well as one of the most politically complex regions—the Balkans—and how the developments that transpired in the early 20th century accelerated the start of the conflict.

The Question of Austria-Hungary

Up until this point, we have not paid much attention to the developments involving Austria-Hungary. In a way, this "prejudice" against the Habsburg Empire is for a good reason. In the "long nineteenth century," as other nations sought to modernize by promoting more liberal views and rapid industrialization, Austria-Hungary was perhaps the loudest advocator and best example of the older, more conservative regimes. The Habsburg royal family, unlike other European monarchies, was unwilling to give up much of the influence and power that they held. The Austrian rulers enacted ineffective measures to combat the empire's problems, which caused Austria to fall behind in development. It was unable to keep up with the standards of modern empires.

Austria-Hungary's structure is crucial to understand. Because of the geographical location of the Habsburg Empire—stretching from the provinces of Bohemia and Galicia of Central Europe to parts of northern Italy and the Adriatic coast of the Balkans—Austria-Hungary was a very complex political entity. Many different ethnicities and nationalities were almost equally prominent.

Different ethnic groups in Austria-Hungary.

https://commons.wikimedia.org/wiki/File:Austria_Hungary_ethnic.svg

By the early 20th century, Austria-Hungary had stopped many of its expansion efforts and had reached the maximum extent of its historical borders. It included many different peoples of Europe: the Germans made up a good part of the population, concentrated in the northwestern regions of the empire; Czechs were prominent in the north, while the Ukrainians and Poles lived predominantly in the northeast; Slovaks and Hungarians dominated the central part; Romanians were focused in the east; Croats and Serbs occupied the southern parts of the empire on the coast of the Adriatic; and finally, although they had a smaller presence than the other peoples, the Italians and Slovenes lived in the western and southwestern parts.

All in all, Austria-Hungary was a geopolitical mess of several European nationalities, which caused an array of problems for the empire time and time again. For example, when new monarchs ascended the throne, their policies could not address the issues of all these different peoples equally. Some parts of the empire felt left out, while others enjoyed more privileges. In addition, most of Europe's transformation since the French Revolution had happened due to the increase of nationalist sentiment that swept through the continent. In Italy and Germany, the majority of the population were ethnically the same. They shared similar cultures, traditions, sets of values, language, and other characteristics that contributed to their efforts of achieving statehood. Austria-Hungary, on the other hand, was not a nation-state, and the nationalist movements in different parts of the empire were crushed time and time again by the royalist forces. The suppression of these movements only caused more discord in Austria-Hungary, requiring stricter measures from the empire, thus sending it into a vicious cycle.

Thus, despite its vastness and past might, Austria-Hungary was plagued by the problems all ethnically diverse empires are eventually doomed to face. It had to concentrate on dealing with the rising nationalist sentiments within its borders, which undermined the centralization of the Habsburg rule and caused the collapse of the empire. Austria-Hungary did not have time or was willing to undertake fundamental transformations. Additionally, it still considered itself an influential player in European power politics, something that mainly derived from its role in the past, although the other European nations knew they were far more powerful and influential than the Austrians by the late 19th century.

The internal instability can be perceived, alongside Austria-Hungary's unfavorable geographical location, as the reason behind its noninvolvement in the colonial game, something that had come to be seen as vital for any empire desiring to be looked at as dominant on the international scene. Austria-Hungary could not even aspire to be a dominant global player if it could not deal with its internal problems first. In a way, the imperialist practices of the other colonial powers were being practiced by Austria-Hungary within its own borders, as the monarchy sought to balance the dynamics between the different struggling nations.

Since internal stabilization was the main factor behind industrialization and rapid development, Austria lagged behind in almost all aspects, unlike its German, British, French, and, to some extent, Russian counterparts. The Austro-Hungarian army was not as professional and disciplined, having been defeated multiple times over the course of the 19th century. Its military technology, strategy, and general outlook on war were not up to standard. Industry and infrastructure were less developed, and Austria-Hungary lacked a competent fleet to challenge even regional rivals. But perhaps most importantly, the monarchy was reluctant to grant more freedom to its subjects.

Chancellor Otto von Bismarck's decision to ally with Austria-Hungary can be justified since Germany was primarily focused on regional security at that time and needed Austria as an ally against France, which was perceived as more powerful and more competent. But as Vienna's only ally diverted its attention to pursue global imperialist endeavors and challenge the British for dominance, it became more difficult for the Habsburgs to keep a firm grip on their subjects. As time would tell, Austria-Hungary, despite its relative backwardness, was indirectly responsible for keeping Europe from bursting into an all-out war. Russia, which was the main regional rival of Austria, was willing to encourage internal conflicts and undermine the Habsburg rule for its own benefit, while France and Britain believed that Germany could not stand a chance against the Entente Cordiale without powerful allies. In the end, the Habsburgs' inability to resolve the tensions within their borders became one of the most prominent causes of World War I.

The Sick Man of Europe

Another formerly great power that played an important role in World War I was the Ottoman Empire. Just like Austria-Hungary, the power held by the Ottomans at the height of their existence was immense; the empire stretched from southeast Europe to Anatolia, the Middle East, and North Africa. But the Ottoman rulers also faced similar problems as Austria-Hungary, resulting in a backward empire on the brink of collapse. In fact, since the Ottoman lands stretched farther than the Habsburgs' domain, they experienced tougher times because they were not able to keep up with industrialization and modernization. Sometimes, the later Ottoman Empire is referred to as the "sick man of Europe," a name first used by Tsar Nicholas II of Russia.

One of the Ottoman Empire's main struggles was the fact it had a different religion from Europe and was perceived as a natural enemy to the Christian Europeans. Although Christianity saw divisions among itself, the Muslim Ottomans were never considered to have been a friend. The clashes between the Europeans and Ottomans were always, in some way or another, a manifestation of the underlying rivalry between Christian and Muslim ideologies.

This proved to be a disadvantage, as the Ottomans had to sometimes face multiple Christian nations at once in battle. For example, during the siege of Vienna in 1683, the Ottomans had made significant progress toward capturing the Austrian capital but were stopped in their tracks after the arrival of a Polish relief force, which forced the Ottomans to abandon the siege and retreat. The Polish had been motivated by the pope to aid Vienna and stop the Muslim invaders. Despite the general disunity of the European nations, they came together time and time again once they realized the Ottoman threat had arrived at their doorstep.

The Ottoman Empire's decline was gradual, starting mainly in the 17th century. When the Ottomans were at the height of their power, no European nation dared to challenge them. Before the Age of Exploration, the Ottomans became the masters of the Mediterranean and controlled much of the trade flow between Europe and Asia, immensely profiting from the trade routes that had to pass through their territories. It was their monopoly over Eastern trade that forced the Europeans to find alternative routes to Asia. They were finally able to circumvent the Ottoman obstacle after they discovered the route around the African continent that led to Asia. Over time, this diminished the Ottoman Empire's economic strength since the European merchants did not have to go through the Turkish lands anymore to reach the rich Indian markets.

In addition to economic struggles, the Ottoman Empire experienced a similar industrialization problem as the Austrians and the Russians. Unlike Britain, France, and Germany, where rapid industrialization had taken off because of the countries' relative stability, the Ottomans did not have the same luxury. Stretched over three continents, the Ottoman Empire struggled to keep order in its distant provinces and was unable to suppress the rebellions that popped up. Out of the major actors of World War I, the Ottomans were the ones who never truly let go of the conservative monarchy. Even Austria-Hungary was less dependent on it. The lack of centralization and the emergence of nationalist sentiments, especially in the European part of the Ottoman Empire, caused many provinces to break off. They were supported by the Ottomans' regional rivals, which wished to see the collapse of a once-mighty empire.

The technological disparities that emerged after the industrialization period also impacted Turkish rule. For instance, European nations adopted new military technologies that gave them a huge advantage over the Ottomans. In fact, much of their strength lay in the size of their armies. The Ottomans were able to muster up armies composed of tens of thousands of men regularly, unlike their European counterparts for much of the late medieval times. Back then, the fate of a battle was largely decided by whichever side had a bigger force.

As time and technology progressed, it became clear that numbers alone did not guarantee success. The Ottoman soldiers were simply outclassed in wars, not only lacking modern equipment to competently conduct battles but also lacking the morale, professionalism, experience, and general discipline of European troops. Its loss in the war with Russia over Crimea demonstrated the disparity that existed between it and the Europeans even more clearly. Everything is relative when it comes to development. The Russian army was never considered to have been up to "true" European standards, but it managed to crush the Ottoman forces relatively easily.

The Balkan Powder Keg

Many underlying problems troubled the Ottoman Empire for a long time. When the European powers noticed their superior position, they actively got involved in the processes that led to the empire's collapse. The Ottoman rule was centralized in Istanbul and the ethnically Turkish Anatolia and Asia Minor, but it was very weak in the peripheral provinces, which seceded from the empire first. The independence movements in Egypt, for example, were quickly supported by the British, who also actively funded the construction of the Suez Canal. The British and French were also increasingly involved in ending the Ottomans' control in regions that were of interest to them due to their proximity to their colonial holdings. Thus, by the late 19th century, Istanbul had lost control of the entire North African coast with the exception of Libya, as well as many of its European possessions. The Ottomans only effectively controlled modern-day Turkey and most of the Middle East.

However, the biggest point of contention between the Ottomans and the Europeans was the Balkans—an ethnically diverse and strategically important region whose developments were influenced by the foreign policies of neighboring empires, namely Austria, the Ottoman Empire, and Russia. The Balkans constituted a natural buffer zone between the Ottomans and Europe, and because the Balkan nations did not enjoy independence, the Ottomans posed a big threat to Europe's security. Each actor saw the region as their own sphere of influence. The Ottomans had controlled most of the region since their early days as an empire, and their claim and ideological strive that they were "European" was heavily based on them being in control of the Balkans. Austria-Hungary was a conglomeration of many nations and included a large part of the Balkan peoples within its borders. The Habsburgs' foreign policy was always based on increasing the empire's reach to rejoin their brothers and sisters who had been left behind, trapped under the tyrannical Muslim rule of the Ottomans. Russia saw itself as a natural leader, a big brother of all ethnically Slavic and Orthodox peoples of Europe, and had tried to increase its presence in the Balkans on multiple occasions. All three sides had their own reasons to challenge each other for dominance in the Balkan Peninsula.

But achieving stability in the Balkans was extremely difficult because of the presence of so many nationalities and ethnicities, each with its own unique identity. Nationalist sentiment was very strong in the Balkan region, and such movements, especially when paired with a rapidly declining Ottoman Empire, saw major success throughout the 19th century. For example, Greece's struggle for independence in the 1820s and the 1830s was supported by Britain, France, and Russia, and the country succeeded in breaking free from the Ottomans in 1832. This weakened the Ottoman presence in Europe and also inspired bordering nations to fight for their own independence.

Serbia gained its autonomy from the Ottoman Empire in 1830. Since Serbia was Orthodox, its independence was guaranteed by Russia. The Russian protectorate proved extremely beneficial, as Serbia managed to achieve territorial gains after Russia's victory in the war against the Ottomans in 1878. Bulgaria was also granted autonomy in 1878. In addition, the autonomous region of Bosnia and Herzegovina was occupied by the Austrians, sandwiching the Ottoman

Balkan possessions between independent states and autonomous provinces.

The Ottomans truly lost their grip over most of the Balkans by 1908, when a major change occurred in Istanbul. The Young Turk Revolution managed to gain a lot of traction since it advocated for the promotion of more liberal values and fundamental changes in the sociopolitical structure of Ottoman life, including granting its provinces more autonomy. In 1908, Sultan Abdul Hamid II was forced to accept the terms put forth by the revolutionaries and reinstitute a constitutional monarchy, giving up much of his privileges as the sultan and weakening Ottoman influence in the Balkan region.

This opportunity was quickly realized by Austria-Hungary, which already saw itself as the rightful ruler of Bosnia, annexing the territory by the end of 1908. The crisis within the Ottoman Empire did not end there, as the country saw itself go to war with Italy just three years later in 1911 over Italy's colonial ambitions in Ottoman-controlled Libya. The Italians wielded a more professional, disciplined, and overall superior army with higher morale. They were able to quickly assume a dominant position in the war and forced Istanbul to give up its control over Tripoli and the rest of the empire's North African possessions about a year later in October 1912.

The Ottomans just could not keep up. The empire's crises never seemed to end. The empire was torn between needing to implement major domestic reforms and spending more resources on keeping peace within its borders. Thus, even before the war with Italy was officially over, the Balkan nations declared war, now united under the banner of the Balkan League, in early October 1912. The Balkan League had been formed after a series of secret negotiations between Greece, Serbia, Bulgaria, and Montenegro. The four former Ottoman provinces signed multiple bilateral agreements that bound each other as defensive or military allies, aimed at keeping themselves safe from the bigger regional threats, namely the Ottomans and Austrians.

Seeing that the war with Italy was going terribly for Istanbul, the Balkan League realized that it was the perfect time to strike against the empire and drive the Turks out of Europe once and for all. The members of the Balkan League were inspired by the nationalist movements of the 19th century and firmly believed they could overcome Ottoman tyranny if they all came together. They devised a plan of action, acknowledging the fact that they lacked the numbers to go up against the Ottomans. However, the Ottoman Empire's main forces were either busy with the Italians or scattered in Asia. Thus, it would take a lot of time and effort for the Ottomans to transport the majority of their troops to the conflict zone, which was not only right at the border of the Balkan nations but also extremely close to Istanbul. The Balkan League decided to strike quickly and decisively.

In early October, the Balkan nations declared war on the Ottomans one after the other and launched a united offensive on multiple parts of Ottoman holdings in the region. Serbia, Montenegro, and Bulgaria led the assaults on land since they fielded the majority of the ground forces, while Greece's main role was to delay the Ottoman reinforcements in the sea since the Greeks possessed a pretty capable navy that was experienced in maneuvering around the area.

The war effort was successful. The Balkan League caught the Turks off-guard and managed to achieve small victories in nearly all the land battles, while the Greeks held off the Turkish fleet in the Aegean and the Mediterranean. The victorious nations signed a peace treaty with the Turks in May 1913, ending the Ottoman presence in Europe after nearly five hundred years. With the Treaty of London, the great powers decided the territorial gains for each participating nation, eventually leading to the creation of the independent state of Albania, the Greek occupation of nearly all the formerly held Ottoman islands, and the clear definition of the borders of the rest of the Balkan states.

With the Ottoman Empire's defeat, the regional balance of power had dramatically shifted once again. But the victorious Balkan nations could not come to terms with the spoils of war, spiraling the region into yet another armed conflict known as the Second Balkan War. Bulgaria declared war on its former allies Greece and Serbia, challenging them for regional dominance. Bulgaria had initially been promised more gains according to the secret agreements prior to the First Balkan War but was left disappointed when the Serbs and Greeks refused to make more territorial concessions. Thus, the Bulgarians invaded, hoping to catch their former allies by surprise. However, they overestimated their own capabilities. Although Bulgaria achieved some progress, it was forced to surrender in thirty-three days, in the summer of 1913. As a result, it lost even more territories to Serbia and Greece and made some concessions to Romania, which had joined the conflict toward the end.

The events that transpired in the Balkans over the 19th and early 20th centuries earned the region an infamous name. By the start of the Great War, the Balkans had a reputation as being one of the most politically unstable locations in Europe. The multitude of ethnically diverse groups with distinct national identities had complicated the political landscape, and while the European superpowers tried to influence the developments in the Balkans time and time again, by the start of World War I, none of them had assumed a dominant position in the region.

Meanwhile, Russia, another interested player in the Balkans, was regarded as the big brother to all the Slavic peoples concentrated in the Orthodox Balkan nations. Russia promoted a Pan-Slavic ideology and supported the independence movements. Strategically, Russia knew that the independence of the Balkan countries would significantly weaken its rival, the Ottoman Empire, and potentially give Russia access to the warm ports of the Mediterranean. Russia also hoped that the instability would be detrimental to Austria-Hungary, another empire that had historically struggled with the Balkan peoples.

Austria-Hungary was put in a very precarious position after the Balkan Wars, as it included a large number of Balkan peoples within its vast borders and was worried that its subjects would also rise up, motivated by their brothers who had managed to achieve independence. The Habsburgs and the newly freed Balkan nations, especially Serbia, did not get along with each other for that reason, and it wouldn't be long until the Balkan subjects of Austria-Hungary started protesting the rule imposed over them by the Habsburgs.

The "Balkan powder keg," as it would be referred to by its contemporaries due to the political instability innate to the region, would eventually decide the fate of the world since World War I would begin shortly after the Balkan Wars. In 1914, the rest of the world truly felt the impact of the Balkan powder keg's explosion.

Part Two: The Outbreak of War

Chapter Five – The Gunshot Heard around the World

It is now time to divert our attention to the events that directly led to the outbreak of World War I and the early stages of the Great War. We have already observed the complicated, competitive sociopolitical climate in Europe by the end of the 19th and the start of the 20th century. Rivals challenged each other at every opportunity, organizing themselves in complex, intricate alliance systems. It was becoming more and more apparent that war was imminent. All that was needed was a spark, something to ignite the tensions between the global superpowers and lead the world into chaos.

As the dwindling Austro-Hungarian Empire tried holding onto its influence over the Balkan nations, complicating the situation even more by trying to exert power, perhaps the most infamous assassination in history would lead to a chain of unfortunate events, eventually ending with the outbreak of World War I.

The Austrian Problem

The Ottoman Empire's decline did not directly translate into an increase in power for Vienna. The emergence of the Balkan nations as independent states posed a threat to the Habsburgs' unity. The Habsburg ruler was worried that the developments immediately on the empire's southern borders would spill over to Austria-Hungary, which included a lot of ethnically diverse groups—peoples whose brothers and sisters had achieved independence and were urging others to join them. The Habsburgs had tried time and time again to deal with the nationality problem, but the measures they implemented were never truly effective, serving mostly as temporary rather than long-term solutions. Austria-Hungary's ruling elite were split between advocating for a federalist system, which would grant a large degree of autonomy for the empire's provinces in return for relative stability, and more imperative measures, such as directly intervening in the political life of their diverse ethnic groups to discourage and punish any nationalist movements.

The developments preceding the Balkan Wars also influenced the dynamics between Austria-Hungary and the newly independent nations. Most importantly, in 1903, the royal Obrenović family of Serbia, which generally had somewhat stable relations with the Habsburgs, was ousted by the Serbian army during the May Coup. The king and queen of Serbia were brutally assassinated, and the Karageorgević family was put in charge. The Karageorgević family's rule was characterized by increased nationalist sentiment, something that led to worsening relations with Vienna and Serbia taking a more pro-Russian course.

For the next few years, Serbia became more and more

involved in the events that unfolded in the Balkans. It tried to increase its borders and muster up a professional army to challenge regional rivals. At the same time, the Austrian annexation of Bosnia and the events of the Bosnian Crisis of 1908 to 1909 left Serbia disappointed and angered because many of the annexed territories were predominantly inhabited by Serbs. Serbian nationalism took off, with the Serbs in Austria-Hungary organizing several secret societies with the aim of promoting nationalist values to achieve liberation while disrupting and undermining Vienna's regime. The *Narodna Odbrana*, which was formed in 1908, is an example of one of these societies. It sought to show that the Serbs did not belong as subjects of the Habsburg Empire.

However, their efforts proved somewhat ineffective, leading to the formation of more radical nationalist groups. These organizations operated largely like terrorist groups, as they planned the assassinations of many Austrian officials. The Black Hand rose to prominence, regarding itself as the next logical evolution of the *Narodna Odbrana*. Its members mainly advocated for the formation of a Greater Serbia—an entity that would include many of the predominantly Serb territories and would be a precursor for an eventual Pan-Slavic state, one led by Serbia.

The Serbian nationalist movements became a significant problem for Vienna. They created instability and encouraged conflict between the subjects and rulers of the empire. If the problem was not addressed quickly, it had the potential, at least in the eyes of the Austrian elite, to cause the complete dissolution of Austria-Hungary. Thus, Austrian statesmen increasingly started lobbying to solve the problem. Among them was Archduke Franz Ferdinand, son of Archduke Charles Louis and the nephew of Emperor

Francis Joseph of Austria. In 1889, due to the untimely death of the heir apparent, Prince Rudolf, and then Archduke Charles, Franz Ferdinand became the next in line for the throne of Austria-Hungary.

Archduke Franz Ferdinand.
https://commons.wikimedia.org/wiki/File:Franz_ferdinand.jpg

Despite having unfavorable relations with the throne because of the issues that had arisen with his marriage, Franz Ferdinand was a prominent figure in the empire and enjoyed a relatively comfortable position of power. This was mainly due to his influence on the imperial military, as he had become the inspector general of the army in 1913. His political views, however, were very different from most of his contemporaries, as he did not really support one side over the other. For example, Franz Ferdinand believed the best way to stabilize the empire was to listen to the ethnic groups and grant them relative autonomy.

He demonstrated more tolerance and sympathy toward some groups, like the Czechs, while frowning upon others, like the Serbs and Hungarians. This assertion mainly came from the fact that he criticized the Hungarian branch of the dual monarchy for its inability to significantly contribute to the empire's joint rule. Archduke Ferdinand also wanted to increase Austria-Hungary's role on the international stage. He believed the empire should be more actively involved in world matters as a European superpower and saw the modernization of the military and the creation of a competent navy as precursors for a more powerful Austria-Hungary.

Archduke Franz Ferdinand was one of the most vocal people when it came to the Serbia problem. His peculiar approach of encouraging a version of federalism without necessarily undermining the monarchy's position was hopeful, as it aimed to achieve the best of both worlds and balance the crisis. However, it was unknown how he would be able to put it into practice. Still, because of the prestigious position Ferdinand was in, he was adamant about adopting a careful approach to Serbia, recognizing that an all-out war would be devastating for both sides.

But despite undoubtedly being one of the most powerful men in the empire, the archduke was highly unpopular. The conservative Hungarians despised him for his federalist views, and many different ethnic groups, including the Serbs, did not support him because they believed his efforts would lead to a pacified nationalist sentiment and stand in their way of reunifying with their brothers and sisters over the border.

The Assassination

So, when Emperor Francis Joseph sent Archduke Franz Ferdinand to the Bosnian capital of Sarajevo to conduct inspections of the imperial army stationed in Bosnia, he arrived at a location where the aggravated public's opinion was largely not favorable toward him. As we already mentioned, due to the significant presence of Serbs in Bosnia, anti-Austrian sentiment had grown, something further instigated by the rise of Serbian nationalist organizations. These groups knew the archduke would visit the capital in June of 1914 and wanted to exploit his visit, planning an assassination to send a clear message to the empire that they were not messing around. In a way, in hindsight, Franz Ferdinand's visit to a place that was so hostile toward him was not exactly the smartest decision.

Several extremist organizations would get involved in planning and carrying out the assassination. Young Bosnia, which was largely comprised of Bosnian-born ethnic Serbs, took the lead. Strongly motivated by popular accounts of heroism from local folklore and legendary historical stories of Serbian heroes, the members of Young Bosnia were eager to put everything on the line to achieve their goal for the greater good, believing that Franz Ferdinand's eventual accession to the throne would end their dreams and hopes for unification. Supplied with arms from the Serbian Black Hand, the assassination plan was put in place.

The day of the archduke's visit to Sarajevo fell on Vidovdan, a Serbian national holiday that memorialized the 1389 Battle of Kosovo between the Ottoman Empire and Serbia. For the conspirators, it was, in a way, symbolic, as a Serb assassin had managed to assassinate the Ottoman sultan back then. They hoped they could repeat the events. Franz Ferdinand was supposed to ride through the streets of Sarajevo with his wife in an open car as part of a motorcade with a police escort. Six assassins knew the predetermined route and armed themselves with hand grenades. They assumed their positions and patiently waited for Franz Ferdinand to pass by.

However, despite the readiness of the assassins, the first attempt to murder the archduke was unsuccessful. The first assassins—Muhamed Mehmedbašić, a veteran Black Hand member, and Vaso Čubrilović—failed to act. Both of them were armed with hand grenades and pistols, but neither of them decided to strike when the motorcade passed them. The next assassin, Nedeljko Čabrinović, was stationed on the opposite side of the road, farther down the route. Čabrinović threw a bomb but missed. The grenade bounced off the archduke's car and fell back onto the streets. It detonated when the next car of the motorcade was on top of it, causing a massive explosion that injured up to twenty people.

Čabrinović saw that his effort was unsuccessful. He popped a cyanide pill and jumped in the Miljacka River, but he survived and was dragged out by the crowd before eventually being arrested by the police. The motorcade realized that the archduke's life was in danger and sped up, breezing past the other assassins without giving them a chance to react. Franz Ferdinand survived the attempted assassination, fleeing to the town hall.

There, the archduke discussed the situation with officers and the governor, expressing his anger over the fact that somebody had just tried to kill him. The parties agreed that the disaster had been avoided, and Archduke Ferdinand, motivated by his wife, decided not to stay in the town hall and pay a visit to those who had been wounded in the attack. The archduke went back to the car with his wife and the mayor, and the motorcade drove off to the nearby hospital. What transpired next is probably the most ironic development that changed the course of the world forever.

In an unfortunate turn of events, the new route that was proposed by Governor Oskar Potiorek was not effectively communicated to the drivers of the motorcade. This meant that instead of altering their route according to the new plan, the drivers proceeded to follow the old route, taking a wrong turn at Latin Bridge. This would prove to be a fatal mistake. After the first failed assassination, one of the assassins, a nineteen-year-old Bosnian Serb student by the name of Gavrilo Princip, decided to abandon his position and move to a local food shop at Latin Bridge, where Archduke Franz Ferdinand was accidentally led to by a mistaken motorcade.

The assassination of Franz Ferdinand.

https://commons.wikimedia.org/wiki/File:Assassination_of_Archduke_Ferdinand.jpg

Once the motorcade took a wrong turn, Governor Potiorek shouted to the driver of the first car from the third car, where he was sitting with the archduke and Duchess Sophia, to stop and back up to the main road. When the motorcade stopped, Princip realized that the archduke was stuck on a bridge just in front of him at point-blank range. He proceeded to fire two shots from his FN Model 1910 pistol, fatally wounding the archduke and his pregnant wife before being immediately seized by the crowd.

Thus, Archduke Franz Ferdinand of Austria had successfully been assassinated by the radical Serb extremists, an event that would have massive implications for the rest of the world.

July Crisis

The assassination of Archduke Franz Ferdinand would eventually cause a chain reaction that would see all the rival European powers go to war with each other, falling like dominoes in a line, with one side dragging the other into the conflict with them. As the next heir of Austria-Hungary, Franz Ferdinand was a very important political figure in Europe, and it was logical that the empire would be aggravated, even though the archduke did not enjoy much popularity. Because of the tense relations between the Habsburgs and the Serbs, the assassination had an even stronger underlying political meaning.

As we have already observed, Austria-Hungary was aiming to spread its influence to the smaller, weaker states of the region. Austria needed an event to justify a potential war, and the assassination of its heir apparent was more than enough. The events that followed Archduke Franz Ferdinand's assassination have come to be known as the July Crisis. Throughout July, different actors tried to justify or prevent war. It would become clear that the balance of power that had been carefully established over the past decades was about to come crashing down.

Although the people of Austria-Hungary were appalled by the archduke's murder, the immediate reaction in Vienna was not what one might expect. Emperor Francis Joseph knew about the region's complex political climate and preferred to conduct investigations about the assassination to determine whether or not Serbia's government had anything to do with it. The interrogations of the arrested assassins determined their Serbian origin, as well as their membership in radical extremist organizations. However, Serbian envoys immediately claimed they had warned Austria-Hungary of the potential dangers associated with Archduke Franz Ferdinand's visit prior to his arrival and also denied that Belgrade had anything to do with the assassination.

By early July, it had become clear that the archduke's assassination was yet another crisis Austria-Hungary had to face. It pointed at the empire's long-standing inability to effectively deal with the upset peoples who dwelled within its borders and posed a legitimate challenge to the Habsburgs' competence. The Austrian government started debating whether or not war with Serbia was a real possibility, discussing the European powers' potential reactions to the conflict.

Serbia was Russia's ally, but would the Russians be willing to support such a small nation and risk fighting an all-out war with the Austrians? If Vienna could successfully expose Serbian involvement in the events that had transpired in Sarajevo, it would have the perfect justification to go to war, and it would be much quicker to conduct a successful offensive. Russia would simply have no time to respond to Austria's actions in Serbia because it was so far away. Plus, Russia's army would need rapid mobilization, something that Moscow was not really capable of doing.

For Austria, localizing the conflict and quickly defeating the Serbs would be the best outcome. It would not only prevent the war from escalating with Russia but also be perceived as a decisive action by Vienna in dealing with the assassination crisis. Still, the emperor chose to wait before making such a major decision, preferring to consult with his military staff and allies.

By the first week of July, Austria-Hungary had gotten the backing of Germany, which pledged to support any Austrian military action against the Serbs. Germany believed that Russia would not pose a threat to the German military. This confidence was justified, as Germany had invested much more in modernizing its forces since the 1870s compared to Russia. The German high command unanimously supported the idea of Austria-Hungary going to war with Serbia and eliminating the newly established nation-state since it would further increase the Habsburgs' presence in the region and weaken Russia. In fact, German officials openly stated that the situation was an opportunity for Austria and declared their firm support for any Austrian action with the infamous "blank cheque," which essentially means that Germany gave Vienna unlimited freedom to solve the crisis.

Still, the evidence of Serbian involvement in the assassination was lacking. Austria-Hungary's cabinet of ministers assembled to properly discuss a joint plan of action. War was certainly popular among the majority, but ultimately, the officials decided to present an ultimatum to Serbia so Austria-Hungary could have a proper, legal justification for war. The main supporter of this decision was Prime Minister István Tisza of Hungary.

The council wanted to present Serbia with a list of demands that would be impossible to meet, a provocative action that would definitely result in war. However, Tisza managed to persuade the ministers to draft another set of ultimatums, a list that would still be harsh on Serbia but still somewhat acceptable to the Serbians. Tisza believed that Austria-Hungary would be in a win-win situation. If Belgrade accepted the terms, it would be seen as a diplomatic feat for Vienna. If the terms were denied, Austria would be compelled to go to war and would most likely emerge victorious. Several versions of the ultimatum were drafted and presented to the emperor. By July 19th, the final draft was ready to be sent to Belgrade.

However, the Austrians decided to wait a few more days. At the time, the French delegation, including President Raymond Poincaré and Prime Minister René Viviani, was visiting Tsar Nicholas II in St. Petersburg. The date of the visit merely coincided with the crisis; it had not been planned as a response to the assassination. Still, the two sides discussed the assassination and the potential of a war breaking out. The Franco-Russian alliance had proven to be beneficial for both sides. France was happy to have friendly relations with Russia because of its reduced international position and saw it as a deterrent against Germany. Russia benefited from the funding provided by Paris to modernize its army, support infrastructure projects, and keep up with the rest of the developing world. President Poincaré assured Tsar Nicholas II that France would commit to the alliance with Russia, even if the situation escalated to more severe levels. The visit proved to be a crucial one, as Russia now had France backing it.

On July 23rd, as the French delegation left St. Petersburg for Paris, Austria-Hungary presented its finalized version of the ultimatum to Serbia. It contained ten points that had to be met by Belgrade within forty-eight hours. If Serbia refused any of the terms in the given timeframe, the Austrian ambassador was to leave immediately and suspend all diplomatic activities. The ultimatum, in hindsight, was unrealistically demanding. It was very unlikely for Serbia or any other sovereign nation to unanimously accept all ten terms. They heavily undermined the Serbian government's power but increased Austria-Hungary's power dramatically.

Serbia needed to suppress all anti-Austrian movements, publications, and teachings and disband nationalist organizations, such as the *Narodna Odbrana*. Austria claimed that the situation in Serbia threatened the empire's security, something that was made clear with the archduke's assassination. The Austrian side also wanted to become increasingly involved in Serbia's sociopolitical processes, demanding that Serbia allow the arrival of Austrian officials to monitor the actions of its government and military and to ensure the elimination of anti-Austrian sentiment. It also demanded the immediate arrest of all suspects involved in the assassination and the start of a new Austrian-led investigation. All in all, the ultimatum was a condescending, humiliating document, the main purpose of which was to assert Austro-Hungarian dominance over the small nation of Serbia and provoke Belgrade into starting a war.

The week after July 23rd saw the whole of Europe in a never-before-seen uproar. Serbia was compelled to respond quickly but knew that accepting the ultimatum would infringe on its sovereignty and set the nation back after successfully regaining independence. Serbia consulted with its ally, Russia, but the tsar was not ready to fully back Belgrade and would only respond if Austria-Hungary acted first. Russia suggested to Serbia that it should accept the terms of the ultimatum or at least partially accept some of the demands and seek an extension of the deadline. Russian foreign minister Sergey Sazonov also tried to persuade the European powers to urge Austria to extend the deadline and requested that Vienna prove official Serbian involvement in the assassination. This request was, of course, denied by the Austrians since they did not have sufficient evidence.

Britain acted as a mediator between Austria and Serbia. Britain's foreign minister was wary of the consequences and recognized that Europe was bound to descend into all-out war if the crisis was not properly addressed. An assembly was convened in London to discuss the matter and determined that the ultimatum would be unacceptable for any sovereign nation. Europe became increasingly worried about the situation's potential escalation.

On the next day, July 24th, Serbia had come to realize that war with Austria was imminent and started to mobilize its army. At the same time, Russia ordered a partial mobilization, influenced by Foreign Minister Sazonov, who had been in talks with the French ambassador to St. Petersburg, Maurice-Georges Paléologue. By that time, the French delegation had not yet returned to Paris, and Ambassador Paléologue urged Sazonov to truly grasp the state of the crisis. Sazonov was convinced that Russian inaction would result in unchallenged Austrian dominance in the Balkans. He persuaded the tsar to order a partial mobilization, despite the fact that most of the Russian ministers believed that Russia was not ready for a full-scale war with both Austria-Hungary and Germany.

Still, perhaps afraid that a potential Austrian takeover of Serbia would be yet another defeat of Russia on the international scene, Tsar Nicholas II was compelled to act, putting the army on high alert. The tsar knew that he had backing from France, having just met the French president, and decided to take a more proactive stance in the Austro-Serbian crisis, even though Russia's military reforms had not been completed yet. The tsar also hoped that the partial mobilization would dissuade Austria-Hungary from immediately declaring war and instead think about solving the matter diplomatically. Instead, it produced a more aggravated response from Vienna, as the Austro-Hungarians, motivated by Germany, realized that Russia was serious.

On July 25th, Serbia officially responded to Austria-Hungary's ultimatum. Although the exact response is not known, Serbia is thought to have accepted all but one or two demands, which were believed to have been a direct infringement on Serbia's independence and sovereignty. The international community received this as good news. Britain believed that Serbia's response was understandable. France and Russia also believed that the Serbian response was more than satisfactory and that Austria-Hungary should not proceed with declaring war. Even Kaiser Wilhelm of Germany, who had been absent all this time on his annual North Sea cruise, stated that Austria should have reconsidered an all-out war and only occupied Belgrade to punish the Serbs and force them to carry out the terms of the ultimatum.

However, Austria-Hungary did not listen to any of these remarks, nor did it really need to. It had the German "blank cheque" and believed that it had a legitimate reason to justify war against Serbia. In addition, Vienna thought that it would act quickly and decisively, eliminating Serbia's army before the bulk of the Russian forces would be able to intervene. And even if St. Petersburg did decide to act, Germany would help in dealing with the Russian forces. Thus, on July 27th, Austria-Hungary finalized its war preparations by mobilizing the army. Germany assured Austria-Hungary of its unshakable position.

By that point, it was clear that war was imminent, but each actor perceived the scale of the coming conflict differently. The July Crisis was still not over, as the next three days would also see critical developments, but after a month of political maneuvering, war could not be prevented.

On July 28th, 1914, Austria-Hungary declared war on Serbia, starting World War I.

Chapter Six – Europe at War

The assassination of Archduke Franz Ferdinand spiraled the European continent into a month of uncertainty. Austria-Hungary, seeking an opportunity to increase its presence in the Balkans, perceived the assassination of its heir as a justification for war with Serbia, despite the fact that the Serbian government had nothing to do with the murder. Throughout July, the blame game Vienna played with Belgrade peaked with Serbia's refusal to accept all of the ultimatum's demands, giving what Austria-Hungary perceived to be a legitimate reason to declare war. However, Austria's perception that the war would be quick and decisive proved to be wrong. Following the declaration of war on July 28th, the rest of Europe would get involved in the conflict, starting World War I.

Europe Enters the War

Despite the remarks of the international community to resolve the disputes with Serbia diplomatically, Austria-Hungary proceeded to declare war and invaded Serbia on July 28th, 1914. After hearing the news, Tsar Nicholas II of Russia ordered his troops to assemble in the four provinces that directly bordered Austria's territories. This was Russia's final effort to dissuade Austria from pursuing an all-out war with Serbia, but it was not successful. The next day, Austrian artillery bombarded Belgrade, causing Russia to fully mobilize its army. Germany ordered partial mobilization. It has to be noted that Tsar Nicholas II and Kaiser Wilhelm II both tried to keep the war from escalating, supporting a peaceful resolution of the conflict. However, their opinions were undermined by the war-hungry military personnel of Austria-Hungary. The German and Russian leaders exchanged a series of letters with each other, exchanging their concerns, but it was too late. The war was already underway.

As Germany and Russia stared one another down and Austria bombarded Belgrade, French President Poincaré finally arrived in Paris from his journey to St. Petersburg. Although he had been somewhat aware of the transpiring situation, he was met with patriotic and anti-German sentiment in Paris. The French urged their president to act decisively. Parallel to Poincaré's arrival, Kaiser Wilhelm II decided to finally mobilize all of Germany's forces, preparing the nation for war on two fronts. The French also responded, demanding that Germany back down, threatening war.

On July 31st, Germany sent out two ultimatums: one to Russia and one to France. Berlin demanded that Russia stop its mobilization and that France declare neutrality in the next twenty-four hours. However, as one would imagine, this was in vain. Russia and France decided to ignore Berlin's demands.

Thus, on August 1st and August 3rd, Germany declared war on Russia and France, respectively. To proceed with their pre-planned offensive, the Germans approached Belgium to let their army pass through neutral Belgian territory to France but were denied. Germany then declared war on Belgium.

Italy, seeing the events unfold and its allies descend into warfare with other major European powers, decided to declare neutrality. The Italians were not required to join the war because the war was not defensive. By the terms of the secret Triple Alliance between Germany, Austria, and Italy, the three powers only had to participate in each other's wars if the war had been declared on them by the enemy. So, because Austria had been the one to declare war on Serbia and because Germany declared war on both France and Russia, Italy did not have to act. Realizing the potential destruction an all-out war could bring, the Italians decided to pursue neutrality.

By August 4th, another major power would enter the war: Great Britain. The British position on the conflict had been made clear; London had urged Austria to resolve the crisis with Serbia through diplomatic means and was generally opposed to war since it was dealing with the Irish independence movement, which had gained prominence in the years leading up to the war. The British Parliament debated Britain's entry into the war for the first few days but was compelled to declare war against Germany after the latter invaded Belgium, whose independence had been guaranteed by Britain. The British demanded the Germans retreat from Belgium on August 3rd, and when they were denied, they officially entered the war on August 4th.

Different powers then proceeded to declare war on each other's respective allies. Austria-Hungary on Russia on August 5th, Serbia on Germany on August 6th, and Great

Britain and France on Austria-Hungary on August 10th and August 12th. This latter declaration of war followed Japan's declaration of war on Germany on August 23rd and the subsequent answer of Austria-Hungary on Japan on August 25th. Austria-Hungary also formally declared war on Belgium on August 28th.

This domino effect seems logical and inevitable in hindsight. Bound by intricate alliance agreements rooted in mutual hatred and national interests, nearly all of the great powers of the world, save the United States and Italy, had joined the war by the end of August 1914. Thus, within two months of Archduke Franz Ferdinand's assassination, the world was divided in two: the German-Austrian axis known as the Central Powers and the Triple Entente of Russia, France, and Great Britain and their respective allies, referred to as simply the Allies. This quick and sharp polarization was a long time coming. The two sides had indirectly challenged each other for decades, avoiding military confrontation in multiple tense instances. Perhaps they were aware of the fact that a potential conflict could reach a previously unseen level.

It is worth taking one last look at the positions of both the Allies and the Central Powers and discussing what exactly was at stake for each nation that had entered the war.

The Central Powers

We have already covered the motivations behind Austria-Hungary's actions. The dual monarchy had experienced tough times after the defeat of Napoleon and the reorganization of the international world order. Austria-Hungary's main problems lay in the fact that the ruling Habsburg family had refused, time and time again, to reduce their own power and allow the implementation of more liberal, democratic practices. By the time World War I broke out, Austria-Hungary was still a conservative monarchy with old standards and beliefs.

The recent regional and global developments affected the effectiveness of the Habsburg rule. Austria-Hungary could not keep up with its European counterparts when it came to modernization. The rise of nationalism directly contributed to the weakening of Austria-Hungary as a political entity—a result that was logical, given the fact that the empire was comprised of multiple nations. These nations, although always having known and practiced their own customs and traditions and spoken their own languages, became increasingly aware of their distinct identities after Napoleon's conquests, igniting nationalist sentiments. In a region as diverse as the Balkans, this proved to be very problematic, as there were many groups yearning for independence.

Austria-Hungary was wary of these developments, recognizing that if it loosened its grip on one nation, letting it break away and achieve independence, it would start a chain reaction that would eventually lead to the dissolution of the whole empire. The Balkan Wars had demonstrated a similar consequence to the Ottoman Empire, another troubled entity that suffered from the same nationality problem as the Austro-Hungarians. The assassination of Franz Ferdinand was an opportunity for the Habsburgs to reassert their dominance and make it clear that they were still strong enough. In a way, one could argue that Austria-Hungary cared little about the international consequences that followed its war on Serbia, focusing only on what the victory in the war would mean for it.

Austria-Hungary's ally, Germany, was in a drastically different position than its southern ally. The German Reich was a direct consequence of nationalism, as this strong sense of German identity had motivated the nation to emerge as a regional and global powerhouse. Having been formed as an independent nation-state way later than its European counterparts, Germany realized early on that to catch up with the rapidly modernizing world, it needed to divert all of its attention to increasing domestic development. Unlike Austria-Hungary, which suffered from having many people groups within its borders, Germany did not have an underlying problem that hindered its rise to dominance. On the contrary, it was a nation-state, meaning that the majority of the population was German and, for the most part, had similar concerns and goals in mind. Germany had great material resources that had not yet been exploited to their fullest extent because of the former disunity of smaller German states. It had an organized civil society and political structure, with a perfectly balanced relationship between the monarchy, the government, and the people. And last but not least, Germany possessed a large, experienced, and disciplined army, one of the best in the world.

Through unification, Germany had all of a sudden been put in a powerful position to challenge its rivals and play a more active role in international politics. By the 20th century, Germany had achieved such substantial progress that it challenged Great Britain as the world's undisputed hegemon. Germany wished to evolve from being the most dominant in Europe to being the most dominant in the world, which contradicted the earlier efforts of Bismarck. The diversion from the Bismarckian course only meant that Germany was left with Austria-Hungary as its ally. Having this dwindling, old monarchy on its side was certainly useful as a deterrent against France, but it was useless for Germany's larger ambitions. On top of this, the rest of the world acknowledged the potential threat of Germany and, led by the efforts of Britain, had come together to undermine it.

By 1914, Germany was aware that it needed to break away from this precarious position and prove its might internationally. Thus, it searched for an opportunity to justify war on its regional rivals. Bound by its old alliance with Austria, Germany realized it could use the assassination to achieve this goal. The Germans were perhaps too confident in their ability to pursue a war on two fronts. They relied on the quick defeat of Serbia by Austria-Hungary's forces and believed they were in a good position to challenge the Triple Entente. Unlike Austria-Hungary, the Germans knew exactly what war on Serbia meant for the rest of the world but thought they had had enough time to prepare for it. Time could only tell if their feeling of superiority over the other nations would be justified or would be yet another instance of overconfidence.

The Allies

The Allied Powers had drastically different motivations. Russia's position was perhaps the closest to that of Austria-Hungary, as St. Petersburg had failed to keep up with the changing times, much like Vienna. With an older political structure and limited channels of political participation, Russia was perhaps the most conservative Great Power at the beginning of World War I. Russia also experienced an ideological struggle. As different monarchs came and left, Russia's perception of itself changed time and time again, with some advocating for Russia to assume a modern European position and increased liberalization, while others wanted Russia to embrace its unique status that incorporated the empire's European and Asian characteristics.

Overall, by the end of the 19th century and in the first decade of the 20th century, St. Petersburg started to perceive itself as the protector of all Orthodox Christian nations in Eastern Europe and the big brother to the Slavic nations that were under Austria-Hungary's and the Ottoman Empire's control. Moscow was seen as the "Third Rome." Enforcing and preserving this attitude of a divine Russian responsibility to exert influence over the Orthodox Slavic nations of Eastern Europe had direct consequences on Russian foreign policy in the early 20th century.

The main point of contention for Russia was the Balkans, a region where many Orthodox Slavic nations were concentrated, giving Russia justification to be involved in their politics and influence major decisions. In addition, Russia was the largest and most populous nation, which gave it constant leverage against its rivals. At times, they were so intimidated by the sheer size and potential of the country that they refused to make any moves against it. However, the size of the empire made cohesiveness difficult, with St. Petersburg stretching its capabilities over two continents. Russia also fell behind in industrialization, as it was still mostly dependent on agriculture and the export of raw materials, both of which were becoming outdated. The other Great Powers had switched to promoting their industry.

Russia was thus a superpower that had not truly unlocked its potential—a factor that served as an advantage and as a disadvantage to its friends and enemies. After having achieved favorable relations with Britain and France and having resolved past disputes with Japan, Russia was more than happy to focus on challenging Austria-Hungary in the Balkans to reassert its dominant position as the protector of the Slavic nations. Protecting Serbia was a symbolic move. In hindsight, if Russia had chosen to let Serbia fight the Austro-Hungarians alone, maybe the whole war could have been avoided. However, to cement itself as a European superpower, Russia firmly believed that it had to be decisive when it came to its sphere of influence.

As we have already mentioned, Tsar Nicholas II of Russia was somewhat hesitant to fully back Serbia against Austria-Hungary and did not believe that risking an all-out war was worth it. However, one of the main reasons behind Russia's decisive position in July of 1914 was France's full support. Despite the fact that the two nations had been allies since their agreement in 1891, the alliance had never truly been tested until Russia decided to directly confront Austria-Hungary. Their alliance dragged France into the conflict in 1914.

The French position is perhaps the most interesting to analyze since the nation had nothing to directly gain from the Balkans. Instead, what France hoped for was to reassert its position in Europe and the world. German efforts to isolate France proved to be pretty successful, as the latter was deprived of any allies for a long time. Everyone was aware of France's might. Napoleon had shown how strong France could be with a competent enough leader with strong backing. In fact, during Napoleon's time, France had the military and economic capabilities to challenge the whole continent by itself.

However, Napoleon's defeat and the redistribution of power were followed by a gradual decline in influence. This became especially clear in the humiliating defeat during the German unification process. The Germans were able to crush the French resistance, reaching Paris. Once there, the Germans signed a declaration for the official formation of the German state, crowning Kaiser Wilhelm as the emperor. In addition to taking away France's prestigious position as the strongest power in continental Europe, Germany also annexed the French provinces of Alsace and Lorraine.

France was then forced to divert its efforts to increase its colonial power. France was still strong in its colonies, arguably the second strongest after Britain, and continued to search for partners on the international stage. Perhaps as a desperate measure, France decided to ally with struggling Russia. At that time, it was clear that France was gambling with its newly gained partner; as we talked about above, Russia was not exactly reliable, lagging behind in development. But if Russia's potential was realized, it could be of help against Germany, which had humiliated and overtaken France as the strongest in Europe.

Thus, in the 1890s and the 1900s, France helped its ally finance many important projects relating to the military, industry, and infrastructure. By 1914, France had made a significant investment in Russia, an investment that had not yet been paid back. Paris believed that the best way for St. Petersburg to pay this investment back would be by taking France's side in a war against Germany. France contributed massively to funding Russian military reforms, which sought to fully modernize all of Russia's army by 1917. France was hoping to get a lot of help in return to undermine Germany's position.

During the Moroccan crises, the situation between France and Germany had deescalated, as neither side was brave enough to risk war over their interests in the colonies. But the opportunity that had arisen with Franz Ferdinand's assassination was too good to let pass. It did not matter for France if Serbia survived or fell. What mattered was a justifiable cause to crush the Germans, and the French did not hesitate.

We have also already addressed the last great European power: Great Britain. Much like France and unlike Russia, Britain had nothing to directly gain by getting involved in the conflict. The smart thing would have been to get away from the imminent explosion of the Balkan "powder keg" and not be consumed by the underlying political tensions that were rooted in the region. In fact, many British officials adamantly opposed intervention in Serbia for that reason, proposing that London should play a passive role and act solely as an intermediary to resolve the conflict between Belgrade and Vienna. In addition, Britain was experiencing a domestic crisis of its own; nationalist sentiment in Ireland had grown, with the Irish demanding more and more autonomy from the British. The tension between those in Ireland advocating for independence and the British government reached alarming levels, providing yet another reason the nation should not have been involved with matters in Eastern Europe.

However, the motivations behind British actions were largely similar to the decisions made by France. Britain had been challenged by the German powerhouse for the position of global hegemon, and it felt that it needed to remind its challenger of its might. Britain could not effectively limit Germany's economic and military advances, but it could rally other great powers under an anti-German umbrella. In the changing times, Britain felt compelled to cling to its position as the strongest in the world, and it would not be able to do so if it let the German machine run rampant over the continent.

This is why the British did not back down from the challenge once Austria-Hungary declared war on Serbia. Britain knew that Germany was strong enough to engage in a war on two fronts and was worried about the consequences a German victory might bring. As Britain saw it, Russia was not ready to withstand a German offensive, and France would eventually fall against a unified German-Austrian effort, even if it could put up a decent fight in the beginning stages of the war. Thus, Britain, much like France, needed a reason to put an end to German domination.

This justification came when Germany declared war on Belgium, a nation whose independence and neutrality had been guaranteed by the Great Powers in 1839 when they all signed the Treaty of London. The treaty bound Belgium to remain neutral in all conflicts but promised that it would never have to worry about a potential war with another Great Power. Germany was very much aware of the treaty when it demanded Belgium grant its forces the right to pass through to French territories. When the request was rejected, Germany declared war, perhaps hoping that Britain would not come to Belgium's defense.

So, by September of 1914, all of Europe's greater powers, save Italy, were at war with each other. The two alliance systems that had emerged in the years prior to World War I to keep each other from escalating conflicts were now involved in armed hostilities against one another. On one side stood the Central Powers: Austria-Hungary, which was desperately trying to keep the empire from crumbling, and Germany, which hoped to finally demonstrate its might as the most developed and strongest nation in Europe. The Central Powers were opposed by the Allies: Russia, which believed it had a moral and strategic obligation not to give up its influence in the Balkans; France, which had decided to honor its alliance with St. Petersburg and stop Germany; and Great Britain, which had come out of its "splendid isolation," recognizing the German threat.

The Great War was underway.

Chapter Seven – The Start of the Hostilities

The Central Powers and the Allies were at war. Both sides were adamant about seeing how the new methods of warfare could influence the outcomes of battles. Military strategists, generals, and soldiers all had their own views and expectations and were eager to test out new equipment on the front lines. Before World War I, the Russo-Japanese War was a clear indication of how things had changed when it came to warfare, and the new opportunities were exciting. However, as the opening stages of World War I would show, much of the military's expectations would be subverted, and the two sides would be shocked, if not disappointed, by the results.

The Cult of the Offensive

In the years prior to World War I, historians have observed a tendency within the Great Powers that has been deemed the "cult of the offensive." Characterized by the glorification of rapid offensive maneuvers rather than defensive warfare, the cult of the offensive can be identified in all the actors of World War I. In fact, some have argued that this cult was one of the principal causes of the conflict's escalation.

The underlying factor of the cult of the offensive is the misconception that was present in Europe with the development of military technology and newly invented armaments, such as the machine gun, different types of rifles and small arms, modernized heavy artillery, and so on. Europeans were correct to recognize that these new weapons were much more powerful than their predecessors, but they wrongly assumed that the advantage would be held by the attacking side rather than the defenders. This misconception was based on the fact that no large-scale conflict had broken out in Europe that was "worthy" of attention. Yes, there was the Russo-Japanese War, which demonstrated the real effects of the new weapons' implementation in battles, but these results pointed to the defender's might; for some reason, this was overlooked. Instead, military personnel believed that in the new age of weapons, the best way to conduct battles would be to try and quickly seize the advantage over the defenders.

The infamous phrase "attack is the best defense" was perceived during this period as a result of the German military's efforts to glorify offensive attacks. In Germany, a nation with arguably the strongest army in Europe by the early 20th century, this view was very much present, with different high-ranking members of the military advocating for a cohesive, rapid offensive with new weaponry.

France and Britain, two nations whose histories had been forged in constant warfare, became obsessed with the narrative of the attacker being more virtuous. British and French officials stated time and time again that their soldiers were suited to conduct decisive offensive operations rather than proceed slowly and wait for the opposing side to attack. They claimed that the justification for this partially derived from the "superior" nature of their soldiers over the enemy, a point deeply rooted in nationalist sentiment. Similar views were even present in Russia and Belgium. Together, these countries assumed that a greater advantage would go to the attackers, who would have higher morale due to their eagerness and perseverance to bravely charge the enemies first. For some reason, offense was synonymized with strength, virtue, and glory, while defense meant cowardness and fear.

It is strange, to say the least, the extent of the Europeans' efforts to glorify offense and discredit defense. If nothing else, throughout most of history, the course of a battle was not solely decided by one side being the first to attack. Many other factors played a significant role in determining the outcome. For example, whichever side had more numbers was usually favored to win, regardless of whether it was attacking or defending. An advantage would often be gained based on the army's position on the battlefield, as terrain and general conditions were important. Not only that, but in siege battles, even after the development of gunpowder and the modernization of artillery, the attacking side was cautious when it came to mounting a full-on assault, as it would result in a lot more casualties because the defenders would shell the approaching troops from fortifications. Instead, waiting out the enemy and depriving them of food and resources was the optimal decision and was pursued in the vast majority of cases.

When taking all of these factors into consideration, it is interesting to see why the Europeans decided to glorify the cult of the offensive and completely disregard defense as a viable battle strategy. As we will discuss later on, the Europeans' keenness to favor the offense would manifest itself in the tactics adopted by the war participants and shape the course of the war, especially during its opening phase. In practice, the cult of the offensive would be proven wrong, as the two sides would be forced to respect the destructive potential of each other's weaponry and adopt a completely new approach to warfare.

The Schlieffen Plan

The European powers had long been developing military strategies in case a war broke out. One such strategy was Germany's Schlieffen Plan, named after the mastermind behind its conception, General Alfred Graf von Schlieffen. In development for nearly fifteen years, from 1891 to 1904, the Schlieffen Plan is one of the most famous tactics of European militarism in the late 19th and early 20th centuries.

The plan itself is relatively easy to understand. Borrowing from the cult of the offensive, Schlieffen's main idea was to find a way to defeat Germany's potential enemies quickly and decisively on two fronts: France and Russia. According to the plan, conducting military activities on both the Eastern and the Western Fronts would be exhausting for Germany, even though the German military was one of the best in the world. If a war broke out on two fronts, the plan suggested to first deal with the French in the West by directing the vast majority of Germany's resources to an all-out offensive on Paris through the Low Countries. Once France fell, Germany would then divert its attention to the Eastern Front, where a large and underdeveloped Russia would not be able to mobilize in time.

The Schlieffen Plan believed that if most of the effort was concentrated on defeating France first, dealing with the Russians would be an easy task since the German military could outclass anything Russia could field in battle. British involvement was also taken into consideration, although not sufficiently enough. When devising the strategy, Schlieffen believed that British intervention, which would come about due to the involvement of the Low Countries, would be too slow and too late. By the time the Brits were able to cross the English Channel with a competent enough force to stop the German advance, Germany would have achieved its goal and defeated the French.

The Schlieffen Plan was very ambitious. Still, the German high command fully believed in the plan's high-risk, high-reward style. Germany thought the plan had taken all of the potential factors into consideration and that its army was capable of executing it flawlessly. Germany believed that it would be able to carry out the Schlieffen Plan without any hindrances. But, of course, it would not be that easy.

Fiasco in Serbia

One other thing the Schlieffen Plan did not take into consideration was the actions of Germany's ally. Austria-Hungary had its own interests that it prioritized over those of Germany, meaning that in order to smoothly carry out the developments outlined by the German offensive, Austria needed to be fully on board. However, as it turned out, this was not the case. The cohesiveness of the Central Powers was crucial if they wanted to see their efforts yield the results they hoped for.

The main problem showed itself at the beginning stages of the war. What were they going to do about Russia? Germany had already proceeded to carry out the Schlieffen

Plan and declared war on Belgium to get to France, focusing most of its strength on the Western Front. This left Austria-Hungary in a weird situation, as Russia was unattended by the Germans on the Eastern Front and threatened the Austro-Hungarians. The Germans had hoped that while they were busy fighting the French in the West, Austria would hold off the Russians in the East. But Austria-Hungary did not move its armies across the border until August 12th, delaying the start of the hostilities and angering Germany. The delay gave Russia just enough time to mobilize whatever it could. The 2nd Austrian Army had to move northeast to support the war against the Russians instead of focusing on taking out Serbia. The situation was very complex, and the efforts of the Central Powers were disjointed.

As a result, three European theaters emerged simultaneously in the first weeks of the war. The Germans fought the combined forces of the French, Belgians, and British on the Western Front. The Austro-Hungarians were trying to break through against the Serbians on the Serbian Front. And the Russians were hoping to undermine the lack of German presence by trying to advance on the Eastern Front.

The main indicator of the Central Powers' incohesive offensive is the disappointing Serbian campaign in 1914. Austria-Hungary had a part of its army depart to aid the Germans in stopping Russia on the Eastern Front, so its efforts to defeat the Serbians proved unsuccessful time and time again in the beginning stages of the war. The Serbs were able to stand their ground against the invaders, proving those who doubted their ability to defend wrong. Serbian commander Radomir Putnik correctly recognized that the Austrians, having split up their forces, were lacking numbers and fully believed that he would be able to keep them at arm's length while aid arrived.

The first battle between the two sides unfolded on August 15th, three days after the Austro-Hungarian armies crossed the border from the north. General Oskar Potiorek of Austria, who was in charge of conducting military operations in Serbia (and the governor who had been with Franz Ferdinand when he was assassinated), overestimated the capabilities of the forces under his command. Perhaps he was eager to win a major battle before Emperor Francis Joseph's birthday and be the bearer of some good news back home. In the Battle of Cer, the first encounter between the Austrians and the Serbs that lasted until August 24th, his forces were not able to break through the Serbian defenses and suffered heavy losses. The Serbians acknowledged that defending the whole border would be in vain and fell back to assume a more advantageous position. After fierce fighting, the Austrians were forced to retreat, marking the first Allied victory in World War I.

The next battles that ensued also saw disappointing results for the Austrian military. In the Battle of the Drina, the Austrians were unsuccessful in trying to cross the Drina River and were forced to retreat, suffering over ten thousand casualties. They had to dig in the trenches and be satisfied with shelling the Serbian positions on the other side. When Austria-Hungary realized that it had weakened the Serbian position through constant bombardment from the trenches, it launched another offensive in early November, forcing the Serbs to retreat at the Kolubara River, where the two sides engaged once again in fierce fighting. By that time, Belgrade was under Austria-

Hungary's control. However, as the Austrians achieved progress, the Serbs retreated farther into their territory, which caused the attackers to feel confident. The Austro-Hungarians chased the Serbians, splitting up their army. The Serbian forces, having just received new weapons from Greece, were able to capitalize on the fact that the bulk of the Austrian army was lagging behind and crushed the Austrian vanguard, something that changed the course of the battle and helped the Serbs achieve victory in several consecutive encounters. General Potiorek was forced to order yet another retreat, giving up Belgrade.

The first Serbian campaign produced disastrous results for the Central Powers. To the surprise of everyone, including the Allies, the Serbians managed to hold off an Austrian offensive on three separate occasions, defending every inch of their lands to the best of their ability. This was even more impressive considering the fact the Serbians did it all alone, without any real help from their allies who were busy fighting on other fronts. Austria-Hungary was disappointed but had not lost all hope. The imperial forces knew the importance of this war and were determined to take out Serbia.

Thus, despite the failure of the 1914 Serbian campaign, it was clear that Vienna was not done. However, this failure was even more catastrophic for the Germans, who were relying on the Austrians to quickly defeat Serbia and then divert the bulk of their forces to fighting Russia on the Eastern Front. The Schlieffen Plan had clearly outlined the objectives of the German offensive and the circumstances in which it would be successful, but one of the most important parts of the strategy—Russia's participation in the war—was becoming more of a problem for Germany. With the Austro-

Hungarians' inability to quickly win against Serbia, Germany was forced to keep a part of its forces in the East, therefore harming its own campaign in the West.

The 1914 Serbian campaign showed that the overly optimistic and glorified cult of the offensive was not rooted in reality and resulted in a drawn-out conflict on multiple fronts for the Central Powers, something that Germany had hoped to avoid.

Chapter Eight – The Theaters of War

As the Serbians were putting up a valiant fight against the Austro-Hungarian offensive, the Germans were trying to break through on the Western Front against the French, Belgian, and British resistance. At the same time, Russia was in the process of mobilizing its scattered forces and preparing to launch a full-scale assault on German and Austro-Hungarian positions. In addition, new theaters of war emerged throughout the world as new actors joined the two sides, seeing the war as an opportunity to achieve their personal interests. This chapter will focus on the major developments in the different theaters of war by the end of 1914 and look at the consequences that followed.

German Offensive in the West

The military activity on the Western Front started as early as August 2nd, when Germany crossed the border of Luxembourg and occupied the tiny nation without meeting any resistance. Luxembourg was just one piece of the puzzle according to the Schlieffen Plan. In fact, the plan had been slightly modified when it came to the details of the German offensive in the West. Although the underlying principle of focusing the vast majority of German forces on taking out France still defined the strategy, the plan had been changed to exclude the invasion of the Netherlands as a means of getting the German army to France.

The Netherlands was one of the three Low Countries, along with Belgium and Luxembourg, and the original Schlieffen Plan envisioned the German army passing through the Netherlands. However, the German general chief of staff at the time of the war, Helmuth von Moltke, modified the plan since the Netherlands was a valuable trading partner. The number of soldiers that would take part in the Western offensive was also lowered, with Moltke firmly believing that more troops would be needed to pursue the war on the Eastern Front due to the Austro-Hungarians' inability to provide support quickly.

After entering Luxembourg, the German soldiers stormed through the Belgian positions, bombarding and capturing a pivotal Belgian stronghold at Liège by August 12th. The German 1st Army took the rest of the Belgian forts relatively quickly, while the 2nd Army followed close behind, reinforcing the German vanguard and securing most of Belgium, including Brussels, by August 20th. By then, only a small part of the remaining Belgian forces had managed to escape and entrenched near Antwerp, while the rest fled to the French border, seeking help from their allies.

The initial stage of the Schlieffen Plan had been carried out. The next stage included quickly overwhelming the French forces from the north and encircling their troops, which were supposed to be defending Paris and conducting their own offensive at the Franco-German border.

France had its own offensive ready to carry out against the Germans. Named Plan XVII, the French offensive envisioned a quick and decisive strike, something that was very much in fashion during World War I, on the provinces of Alsace and Lorraine, which Germany had annexed during the War in 1871. With similar ambitions as the Schlieffen Plan, Plan XVII dictated the French efforts of armament and mobilization in the two-year period leading up to the war. With everything in place, the plan was set into motion parallel with the German invasion of Belgium on August 14th. Nineteen French divisions crossed the border into Lorraine to mount a rapid attack on the German positions.

However, the French efforts were disastrous, especially when compared to the Germans' success. The German 6th and 7th Armies had anticipated a potential French assault and were lying in wait with their positions heavily fortified when the French attacked, crushing them in the battle of Morhange-Sarrebourg a week after the French troops crossed the border.

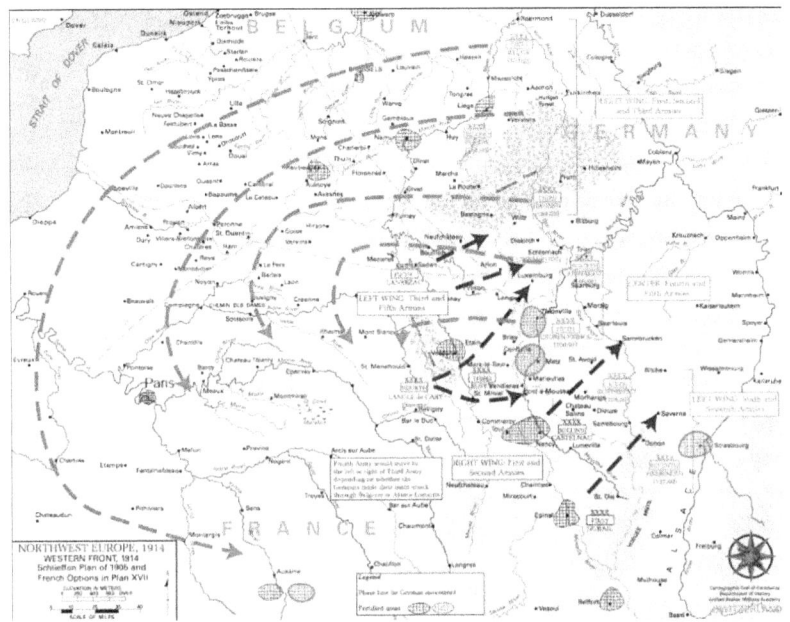

The Schlieffen Plan and Plan XVII.
https://commons.wikimedia.org/wiki/File:Schlieffen_Plan.jpg

In an interesting turn of events, the French advances in German territories managed to tempt General Moltke to alter the Schlieffen Plan. Germany was aware that France would have likely tried to break through to Alsace and Lorraine, so to counter this, the Germans decided they would not engage in an all-out battle with the French to fully drive them out. Instead, the Germans would retreat after dealing significant blows to the French forces. Then, according to the Schlieffen Plan, once Germany emerged victorious in Belgium, it would send its forces to wrap around the French positions from the north to encircle the bulk of the French forces.

However, Moltke did not expect the French to accept the German bait so naively. Seeing that the French troops had thrust deep into the German positions but had not achieved any significant victories and suffered a lot of casualties,

Moltke diverted six German divisions from the Belgian wing to attack the French at Lorraine. This move directly clashed with the intended outcomes of the Schlieffen Plan. The Germans dealt heavy losses to the attacking French and forced them to retreat from Lorraine, but they achieved it by sacrificing the cohesiveness of the Schlieffen Plan, weakening their own wing in the north that was supposed to deal the decisive blow to Paris.

The fighting that ensued in the first month of World War I on the Western Front is collectively referred to as the Battle of the Frontiers. Germany successfully surmounted the Belgian resistance and entered France from the northeast, while the French tried to break through to its long-lost provinces of Alsace and Lorraine on the Franco-German border. Over two million soldiers participated in this group of engagements. The Allies suffered over 300,000 casualties, while Germany lost about half of its troops. By late August, the French advance in Lorraine had been halted, and the German armies had secured a safe passage to northeastern France through Belgium.

The international community was shocked, not because of Germany's success but of the wicked ways in which the Germans treated the defeated Belgians. The Germans set fire to several towns and executed hundreds of civilians. They were accused of committing war crimes and atrocities that did not serve the purpose of emerging victorious in war. "The Rape of Belgium," as the German actions would come to be known, significantly damaged Germany's image, with anti-German sentiment rising across the nations that declared neutrality. This sentiment was further propagated by the Allies.

All Quiet on the Western Front

To salvage the relatively unsuccessful French offensive, French General and Commander-in-Chief Joseph Joffre decided to launch a counteroffensive on the German positions in the northeast with his troops in the south. General Joffre was hoping for aid from the British, who had sent an expeditionary force to get involved in the war. Supported by the BEF (British Expeditionary Force), the 3rd, 4th, and 5th French Armies led an attack on the Germans south of Liège but suffered a crushing defeat. Underestimating the German numbers, the French and British were trapped between the enemy forces, forcing General Joffre to order a retreat to save as many troops as he could. This defeat was followed by a retreat of all Allied forces, even the ones that had made headway in Lorraine.

Plan XVII was completely abandoned in favor of a new strategy. Joffre tried to reorganize the Western Front, giving up a significant part of northeastern France to the Germans, who had already established their presence in the region, and setting up a new united front. Joffre concentrated the majority of the Allied forces tens of kilometers northeast of Paris in the area around the Marne River, where they assumed a defensive position.

Still, the German advance would not have been fully overcome by the Allies if it wasn't for miscommunication between the German officers. As the Allies reorganized their forces under General Joffre's orders, Germany was slowly closing in on Paris, trying to gather up the remainder of the troops from the northern wing to join together for a united offensive and the final stage of the Schlieffen Plan. Following their mass retreat from the frontier, the military governor of Paris, Joseph Gallieni, was charged with creating a plan to defend the French capital and its outskirts. At the same time, Commander Moltke ordered the German 1st and 2nd Armies to join up under the command of General Alexander von Kluck. However, due to a communication error, Kluck proceeded to change the direction of his forces, marching them northeast of Paris in the valley of Marne instead of southwest, abandoning the original plan that sought to fully encircle the French capital. This meant the German army under Kluck had exposed its right flank, providing an opportunity for the Allies to strike.

The Allies sought to be the first to encircle the enemy, and their counteroffensive started on September 4th when Governor Gallieni convinced Joffre to try and exploit the German position. The First Battle of the Marne, as it would come to be known, would last from September 6th to September 12th and would catch the German forces off-guard. The opportunity was successfully seized by the united French and British armies, as they managed to split apart different German divisions and quickly overwhelm them. The Allies risked exposing new flanks of the German forces, so the Germans decided to retreat and abandon their initial plan of encircling Paris.

In addition to the risk of getting flanked, which would mean fighting with a constant disadvantage due to disrupted supply lines, the German forces were also exhausted from their continued advance through Belgium. They were pretty deep in Allied territory, and suffering a heavy defeat would detrimentally affect German morale. Thus, the Germans retreated, digging in at the Lower Aisne and successfully withstanding the following Allied offensives. The Battle of the Aisne demonstrated that the power dynamics in trench warfare were swayed in favor of the defenders. They enjoyed a much safer position when compared to the attackers, whose only move to break through was to charge head-first at the entrenched soldiers while being subjected to heavy machine gun and artillery fire.

Thus, the repelled German offensive on Paris was followed by a failed Allied counteroffensive. Both sides had exhausted their resources, and neither had the capability to break through. So, instead of trying to engage in full-on frontal combat, which would not have been beneficial for either side, the Germans and the Allies instead tried to outflank each other. This produced what is now known as the "Race to the Sea," as both sides maneuvered their forces from northeastern France all the way to the North Sea in the hopes of catching the other off-guard and exploiting a potential gap by flanking the enemy. In the span of a month, the two sides dug a complex network of trenches that ran parallel to one another from the North Sea all the way through northeastern France to the Franco-German-Swiss border.

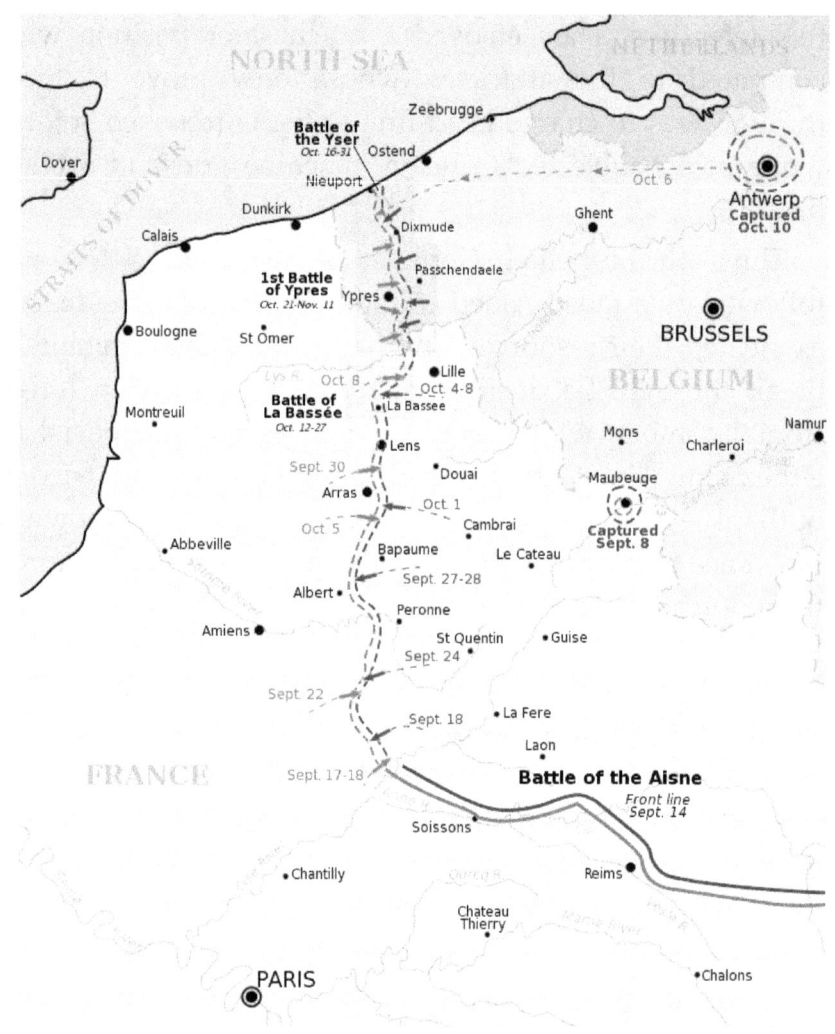

The Race to the Sea.

https://commons.wikimedia.org/wiki/File:Race_to_the_Sea_1914.png)

By December 1914, the military confrontations between Germany and the Allies had largely died out. The two sides had established two opposing trench systems, and neither wished to make the first move to try and break through, knowing that any efforts to overwhelm the other side's position would only end in disaster. While the Schlieffen Plan had seen partial success, the French were unable to mount a significant counteroffensive in line with their original Plan XVII. Still, the Allies had managed to prevent the fall of Paris and driven the Germans out of the immediate vicinity of the French capital with the Battle of the Marne. This meant the Allies' morale was still somewhat high on the Western Front.

On the other hand, Germany had seen success against the Belgians. Only Antwerp was effectively under Belgian control, with the Belgians surrounding the city with trenches. The Germans had also taken control of a large portion of northeastern France—a piece of land that produced much of France's coal and steel, affecting the French war effort.

In the opening months of World War I, the Allies in the West suffered up to a million casualties, with over 300,000 dead soldiers and 600,000 wounded, while the Germans had suffered about 200,000 less in total. What followed the chaotic and bloody developments of the first months on the Western Front was years of stalemate, with the other theaters of war being of more interest. The Western Front, with the entrenched Germans on one side and the British and French on the other, saw no real action for the remainder of World War I. The iconic novel by German writer Erich Maria Remark, who served on the Western Front during the war, perhaps best describes the situation that ensued after the two sides entered a long stalemate: it was all quiet on the Western Front.

The Bear in the East

The war on the Eastern Front developed quite differently. Russia was supposed to launch an offensive on the Central Powers to help relieve some of the pressure on the Allies in the West. However, as we already mentioned, the Russian military reforms that were funded by France had not yet been fully completed, meaning that much of Russia's vast army was not quite ready to fight. The Russian troops were scattered all around the country, and their hasty mobilization was not nearly as cohesive as the Germans, who, according to the Schlieffen Plan, had adopted a defensive approach toward the Russian threat during the opening stages of the war. Germany believed that with the help of Austria-Hungary, Russia would not be able to achieve meaningful success on the Eastern Front. The Germans were fully confident that they would have enough time to transfer a large part of their forces from the Western Front to the East.

But to Germany's dismay, things did not go according to plan. Despite seeing initial success, the Germans could not finish off the Allied resistance in the West, instead forcing a stalemate, with the two sides staring each other down from the trenches. Germany had to constantly keep a significant part of its force on the Western Front since there was a realistic chance of an Allied counteroffensive, which would have been enough to overwhelm the German positions and nullify their progress. In addition, Austria-Hungary faced resistance in Serbia. Since it had not taken out the Serbian forces, it could not contribute an adequate number of troops to battle Russia. By the end of 1914, Austria-Hungary had not made any real progress against Serbia. It split off its army to help Germany defend against Russia and, in turn, requested Germany's help with invading the Serbs.

However, this disadvantage was leveraged by the fact that Germany's army proved to be superior to Russia's army. It was better equipped, demonstrated more bravery, and had higher morale compared to the Russian forces. In nearly every encounter, the Russians had to rely on superior numbers or the element of surprise to achieve any success. And even then, they would still lose tens of thousands of soldiers every time they approached the Germans because of the latter's more advanced artillery. Unlike the Western Front, where entrenchment resulted in a deadlock, giving the defenders a massive advantage, the German army was so superior to the defending Russian forces that the trenches did not slow them down as much. The Russians were also plagued with problems of overextension and disrupted supply lines. The Russian army was probably a better match for Austria-Hungary. When these two nations clashed in the southern parts of the Eastern Front, Russia did see some success.

The Fight for East Prussia

The war in the East between Russia and the Central Powers unfolded separately in two different locations. One part of the Russian army launched an offensive on East Prussia and fought off the Germans, while the other half of the mobilized Russian forces held up the combined Austro-Hungarian and German forces in Russian Poland. The Russians did see initial success against the Germans, who suffered defeat in the Battle of Gumbinnen on August 20th, 1914. Three days earlier, a quick strike by the German vanguard at the Battle of Stallupönen yielded no significant results for Germany, although it did provide some intel on the intended route the Russians planned to take. Paul von Rennenkampf and Alexander Samsonov led the Russian 1st and 2nd Armies, respectively, in a combined effort to overwhelm the German defenses in East Prussia. Instead of solely acting defensively, Maximilian von Prittwitz, who was in charge of the German forces, hastily decided to attack the Russian armies while they were recovering from the initial blow of the Germans, but his attack was repulsed. Seeing that Samsonov's troops could converge on his position, Prittwitz ordered the Germans to retreat.

Two days later, Chief of Staff Moltke decided to replace Prittwitz on the Eastern Front, believing that the latter had been consumed by panic after suffering defeat and having to retreat. He placed Paul von Hindenburg and Erich Ludendorff in charge of the German 8th Army in East Prussia, confident that the experience of these two commanders would turn the tides in their favor. This decision proved to be extremely successful. After having achieved victory, the Russian 1st and 2nd Armies threatened the capital city of Prussia, Konigsberg, and Moltke knew that letting the enemy take the city would shatter the soldiers' morale. Konigsberg was a historical military hub and held symbolic value to the German troops, most of whom were from East Prussia.

So, instead of falling back and allowing the two Russian armies to join up, Hindenburg and Ludendorff decided to launch a counteroffensive and converge on the 2nd Russian Army under Samsonov. Having intercepted Russian communications and utilizing the local railway systems for quick maneuvering between positions, the Germans devised a plan to overwhelm Samsonov's left flank, relying on the element of surprise to crush the Russian advance.

Paul von Hindenburg.
https://commons.wikimedia.org/wiki/File:Paul_von_Hindenburg-2.png

In a five-day battle that began on August 26th, the Germans perfectly carried out their plans. The rapid attacks on Samsonov's massive army, which in total counted about 230,000 troops, could not be answered by the Russians. By splitting off a part of the German forces to delay the 1st Russian Army, Hindenburg and Ludendorff managed to shatter the morale of Samsonov's soldiers, who started retreating despite having numerical superiority. The Germans were able to effectively exploit every opportunity that presented itself in their favor and achieved a decisive victory.

By August 30th, the Russians had lost a majority of their initial forces, with more than eighty thousand killed or wounded. Even more were taken by the Germans as prisoners of war. On the other hand, the Germans only suffered thirty thousand casualties at most. This piece of military brilliance has come to be known as the Battle of Tannenberg and had immense implications for the war on the Eastern Front. Samsonov, who had managed to escape the slaughter, committed suicide, ashamed of his defeat. Devastated by the defeat, the Russian high command tried to hide the news of the battle from the public, afraid that an already strong anti-war sentiment could grow to new limits and cause an array of internal problems.

The Germans were able to convert the victory at Tannenberg into another successful offensive against the Russian 1st Army under Rennenkampf in the northern part of East Prussia. Being in better shape and in a better mood from defeating the 2nd Army under Samsonov, Field Marshal Hindenburg and General Ludendorff ordered their troops to prepare for another attack. The Germans wanted to force a general Russian retreat from their territories. Their goal was achieved with the Battle of the Masurian Lakes, which lasted from September 4th to September 13th. The German army managed to successfully catch the Russian 1st Army off-guard and completely surround it. The Germans' main advantage was the region's railway network, which enabled the rapid transportation of troops and supplies. The Russians' numerical advantage did not amount to anything in this case either, as they were forced to retreat back to the border and leave the German territories.

In the fight for East Prussia, Russia suffered more than 230,000 casualties, with about 100,000 men taken as prisoners. The German losses were probably a third of that number. In the end, despite seeing some initial success, the Germans were able to successfully repulse the Russian advances with competent leadership and buy time for their armies in the West.

Galicia

East Prussia was not the only region on the Eastern Front where fighting unfolded in the beginning months of World War I. Clashes between the Central Powers and Russia also took place in the province of Galicia. A province historically populated by ethnic Slavs, Galicia was right on the border of Russia, making it an easy and logical target for the Russian forces. The Austro-Hungarian efforts to defend the province seemed disjointed and incoherent, as the imperial army was also busy fighting in Serbia, a fight that cost them much time and resources in the war's opening stages.

Realizing the importance of Galicia as a gateway that connected Russian Poland with the heart of Austria-Hungary, both sides thrust into the province with whatever strength they could. Of the mobilized Russian forces, nearly half of them were sent to fight in Galicia, with the Russian 3rd, 4th, 5th, and 8th Armies counting about a million soldiers combined. They heavily outnumbered the Central Powers when fighting began in late August, as Germany had sent most of its troops to the West and only had its 8th Army in East Prussia. The Austro-Hungarian forces were mobilized mostly against Serbia. Still, in true fashion of the over-glorified cult of the offensive, Austrian Chief of Staff Franz Conrad von Hötzendorf believed the best way to stop the Russian advance was to confront them directly and be the first ones to strike instead of trying to delay before help arrived. Thus, the Austrian 1st, 3rd, and 4th Armies waited for the Russians to approach Galicia, spreading out to cover a front over 240 kilometers (149 miles) long.

In late August, the two sides clashed relentlessly on several different occasions. Unlike East Prussia, where the Germans had a more advanced army than Russia, the latter's strength was almost evenly matched with the Austro-Hungarians. In fact, because of numerical superiority, the Russians were able to swing the battles in their favor multiple times. Initially, however, the Austrians were successful, as they managed to defeat the Russian northern flank in the battles of Kraśnik and Komarów, inflicting heavy casualties and taking more than twenty-five thousand men as prisoners.

But these efforts were undermined when the Russians achieved victory at the Battle of Gnila Lipa, where the Russian 3rd and 8th Armies crushed the attacking Austrians. By August 30th, after two days of fighting, the Russians were able to drive the Austrians back, forcing Commander Hötzendorf to recall his northern force to reinforce the Austrian center and south. However, this was not enough, as the Russian forces that had retreated in the north rejoined with the 3rd and 8th Armies and launched a massive counteroffensive that lasted a week, from September 3rd to September 10th. They were able to exploit the fact that the Austrian army was not united, picking it apart in the Battle of Rawa and forcing an all-out Austrian retreat from Galicia. The Russians captured more than seventy thousand prisoners.

In the Battle for Galicia, the Russians managed to advance in Austro-Hungarian territory by about 160 kilometers (99 miles). Crucially, they managed to take the important city of Lemberg, which reassured the Russian public, which had grown increasingly upset over the Russian losses in East Prussia. By mid-September, the Russians had managed to inflict an estimated 370,000 casualties to the Austrians, including more than 100,000 soldiers captured as prisoners of war, while suffering about 250,000 themselves. It was an important psychological victory for the Russians too. They hoped to continue their successful advance against the Austro-Hungarians to recoup their losses against Germany in the north.

Russia's success was certainly concerning for the Central Powers, to say the least. For Germany, it was vital that the Austro-Hungarians hold up the Russians as the Germans dealt with France in the West, but the Austrians' inability to stop the Russian advance required extra German attention. The Russian army, on the other hand, had successfully pushed the Austrian resistance to the Carpathian Mountains and continued their efforts to take more of Galicia. Immediately after taking Lemberg, the Russian armies converged on Przemyśl. With over 300,000 troops, the Russians laid siege to the town, which was garrisoned by about 130,000 Austro-Hungarians. The siege would last for more than six months.

Losing Przemyśl would be a disaster for the Central Powers, as Russia would have weakened their positions and threatened the German province of Silesia, which was an industrial hub and necessary to continue the war effort. After Russian General Radko Dimitriev's initial attempts to storm the fortress ended with about forty thousand casualties, the Russians decided to take a slower approach and wait out the surrounded city, which, in addition to the army, housed up to twenty thousand civilians.

After seeing that the Austrians could not hold out against the Russians for much longer, Germany decided to transport a significant number of its forces to Galicia to help its ally. Having achieved a decisive victory at Tannenberg and having driven out the Russians from East Prussia, Field Marshal Hindenburg felt confident that, with German aid, the Central Powers would be able to surmount the Russian resistance and prevent them from advancing. The Germans and Austrians decided to strike together, but the Russians were still able to defeat them at the Battle of the Vistula River, near Warsaw, a battle that lasted for most of October.

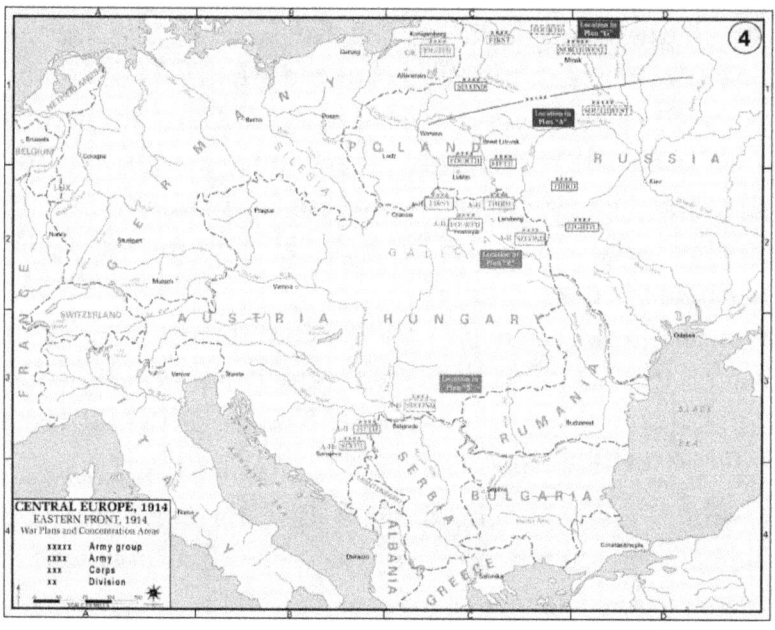

Eastern Front, 1914.

https://commons.wikimedia.org/wiki/File:Eastern_Front,_1914.jpg

Despite their inability to break the Russians, the Central Powers inflicted 150,000 casualties to the enemy while suffering about 70,000 of their own. This engagement was another example of the two allies' inability to properly coordinate, as they both blamed each other for the defeat, saying that their retreat was only a strategic move to assume better defensive positions and await the Russian advance. The victory at the Vistula River filled Russia's army with confidence. The soldiers and officers naively believed they were capable of beating Germany despite the obvious disparities between the two sides. In the long term, the Russians' overconfidence would have detrimental effects on their campaign of Prussian Silesia.

Part Three – 1915–1916

Chapter Nine – New Players, New Developments

The opening months of the war saw many interesting developments that challenged the preconceived notions held by the participants. Although the cult of the offensive had been disproven wrong, with the first battles of the war strongly suggesting that head-first strikes only meant thousands of casualties for the attacking side, the warring nations were still confident in their abilities and tried to follow their war plans to the fullest extent with rare exceptions.

In Europe, the war had unfolded in unexpected ways, with Germany unable to achieve the intended outcomes of the Schlieffen Plan, Austria-Hungary foiled in Serbia, and Russia making partial progress on the Eastern Front. However, as the months passed, new actors began to enter the war on both sides, something that truly gave the conflict the fitting title of a "world war."

The Ottoman Entry

The Ottoman Empire, as we previously discussed, was in a tough situation before World War I broke out in 1914. In fact, the Balkan Wars, which heavily affected the "sick man of Europe," were an indirect cause of World War I. The Ottomans had not only lost a lot of territories and resources with the events of the First Balkan War, but the defeat had also taken away Turkish pride. The world now knew that the Ottoman Empire was weaker than ever, so weak, in fact, that several small nations were able to easily achieve victory against it. The empire was also undergoing a massive political and cultural revolution, which contributed to the development of a new Turkish identity, one based largely on irredentism. The Young Turk government, which had been in power since 1909, advocated for modernization and the spread of more democratic values. But by the start of the war, the Ottomans were still in a deep political crisis. The country was also viewed unfavorably by almost all of the European powers, with Germany, France, and Britain all turning down the Ottoman Empire's offers for an alliance by 1911. Bulgaria was the only nation that accepted an alliance with Constantinople, doing so in August 1914.

However, when the war broke out, the Great Powers' perception of the Ottomans started to change. The empire still had a large military, and it bordered the war's participants in different regions. It was very close to the Serbian and Eastern Fronts, directly bordered Russia with the Caucasus, and shared borders with Britain in the Middle East and India. Even though Constantinople had officially declared neutrality in the first few days of the war, it became clear to the nations that having a favorable relationship with the Ottomans could potentially swing the tides. Thus,

Britain and Germany increasingly started lobbying the Ottoman government. In the end, Germany gained the upper hand by "selling" two German warships, the *Goeben* and the *Breslau*, with German crews to the Ottomans. The Turkish government also adopted an increasingly anti-British stance, provoking Britain on multiple occasions and rejecting British requests regarding naval activity in the Mediterranean. In September, it became clear that Constantinople was a German ally, as it closed the Turkish straits that linked the Black Sea with the Mediterranean, inflicting a massive blow to the Russian economy and further infuriating the Allies.

The Turkish government debated on whether or not to enter the war. The German warships signaled that Germany wanted the Ottomans on its side. The pro-British and the pro-German debate in the Ottoman parliament ended in favor of the latter, and by October, the Ottoman government had made up its mind to join the Central Powers. This meant the Ottomans would most likely be confronted by resistance on different fronts, especially in Egypt and on the Turko-Indian border.

The leader of the Young Turks, Enver Pasha, hoped that by the time Britain would be able to respond, the Turkish and Austro-German forces would have diverted all of their strength to defeating Russia, giving them time and resources to deal with the Brits. In late October, led by the German *Goeben*, the Turkish fleet sailed up the Black Sea and started bombarding the Russian port cities, including Odesa. Russia swiftly declared war on November 1st, and the rest of the Allies followed suit in the next three days.

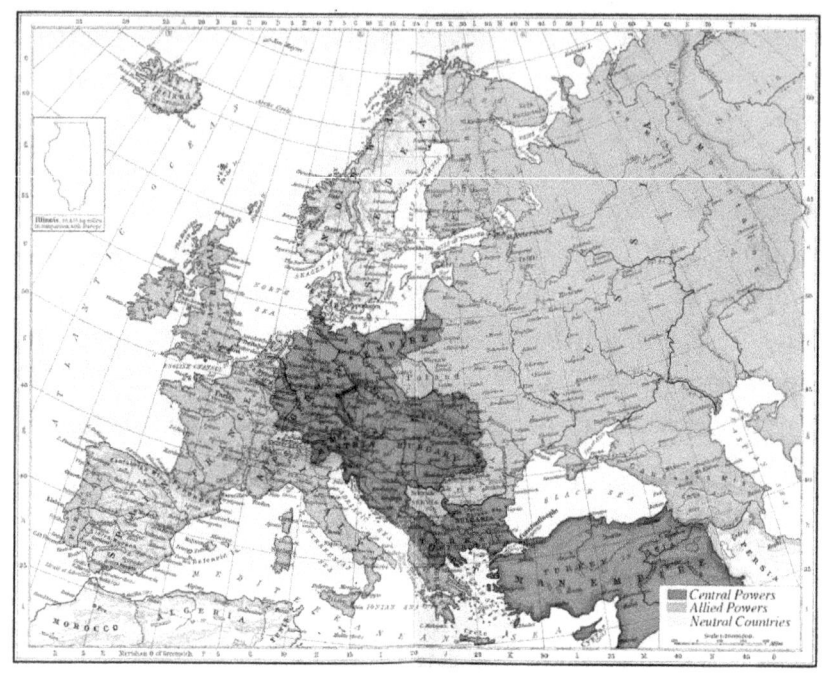

Europe and the two alliance systems by the end of 1915.
https://commons.wikimedia.org/wiki/File:Map_1914_WWI_Alliances.jpg

In a shocking move that showcased Germany's diplomatic brilliance, the Central Powers now had manpower from Turkey to hold up the Allied forces on different fronts and leverage their advantage by creating more problems for Britain. As for the Ottoman Empire, the sick man of Europe, the war promised payback from the disasters of the Balkan Wars, with Constantinople hoping to receive a significant portion of Russian- and British-held lands in the Caucasus and Asia.

Gallipoli

The Ottoman entry into World War I resulted in interesting developments all around the world, the most famous of which was the Allied campaign at Gallipoli. In January 1915, Russia urged Britain to do something about the Ottomans, as the latter had increasingly pressured

Russia with its blockade of the straits and constant bombardment of Russian ports. The British had been debating the right course of action to further weaken Germany's position since the Western Front had come to a stalemate. Forced to act to relieve pressure on Russia, which had been fighting alone for almost six months against the Central Powers, the British high command devised a plan— a naval expedition into the very heart of the Ottoman Empire. According to the plan, the British would sail to the Gallipoli Peninsula, a small area on the western bank of the Dardanelles, and try to take it. If they were successful, they could establish a secure spot for future operations and put British troops dangerously close to Constantinople.

In February 1915, the British Royal Navy set out on one of the most ambitious landing operations in its history. The naval bombardment began on February 19th when a combined Franco-British navy opened fire on the defenders' positions. But this resulted in no real progress, as the Turkish defenses still stood strong after a week. The Allies were dissatisfied with the results, and Winston Churchill, First Lord of the Admiralty, urged the fleet's commander to increase his efforts and pressure the Ottomans.

The main problem was the area's awkward geography. The Dardanelles Strait was pretty narrow, and it was hard for large ships to effectively maneuver through it. In addition, the banks of the sea were hilly, giving the defenders a massive advantage since they could set up their forts and trenches along the high ground and answer the Allied navy with machine gun fire.

Thus, no progress had been made by March. In mid-March, the Allies sent eighteen warships to the Dardanelles. This also yielded no results, as the increased number of warships only made it harder for them to move around and dodge the mines. The Allies had managed to exhaust the defenders' resources by the end of the month but were reluctant to continue their efforts and recalled the naval forces by April.

This did not stop the Allies from devising a new strategy for Gallipoli. They envisioned landing on the peninsula instead of utilizing constant naval bombardment. Britain, demonstrating its true colonial power, transported trained troops from Australia and New Zealand to Egypt, organizing them into the combined ANZAC (Australian and New Zealand Army Corps) to use in the campaign. In total, the ANZAC counted about sixty thousand men. The bulk of the landing force was comprised of 345,000 soldiers from the British Mediterranean Expeditionary Force and 70,000 soldiers from the French Oriental Expeditionary Corps. Together, the Allies decided to land at every possible point on the Gallipoli, hoping to disorient the defenders and overwhelm them with their superior numbers.

French troops landing at Gallipoli.

https://commons.wikimedia.org/wiki/File:Landing_French-Gallipoli.jpg

Thus began the biggest amphibious landing operation in history, with the ANZAC forces successfully breaking through and landing at a small cove on the Aegean side of the Gallipoli Peninsula, fittingly nicknamed "ANZAC Cove." The Turkish machine gun fire made it hell for the colonial forces to achieve their intended objectives, but by nightfall on April 25th, the ANZAC had managed to set up a small beachhead and awaited further orders. At the same time, the main Allied army tried to land at five different points around Cape Helles, of which three attempts were successful. The advantage that the defenders held proved to be too much for the Allies to overcome, though. They made no significant advances on the Turkish positions in the first few days.

The Allies asked for reinforcements, but the beachheads they had established were too small for more troops to arrive. So, the soldiers that had landed on the peninsula were forced to dig in to avoid Turkish fire to the best of their ability. The British high command was indecisive when it came to the next stage of the operation. Every time the Allies tried to break through, they suffered thousands of casualties. Back in London, after fierce debates, it was reluctantly agreed that the operation would continue. New troops were sent to reinforce the landing in the summer of 1915. The reinforcements also managed to establish a beachhead in the northern part of the peninsula in August at Suvla Bay. Still, the combined offensive yielded no significant results for the Allies, who had not seen any real progress anywhere else by mid-1915 either. So, after further discussion, the Allied high command decided to fully call off the operation and evacuate all the soldiers who had landed on the beaches by January 1916.

It was a painful decision and a disastrous development for the Allies, who lost more than 250,000 men in the whole campaign, with about 60,000 dead and the rest injured or sick. As time would show, the whole operation was poorly planned, and the cult of the offensive once again proved ineffective. The Ottomans managed to hold out thanks to the defenses they had set up around the hills on Gallipoli. They suffered about the same number of casualties themselves, but at least they managed to dissuade the Allies from continuing their efforts and kept the heart of the empire—Constantinople—safe from the enemy.

Interestingly, not all historians regard the Gallipoli campaign as a total fiasco, with some believing that the Allied efforts to land on the peninsula distracted a significant number of Ottoman troops from being involved in other theaters.

New Frontiers

With the Ottoman Empire's entry into the war, several new frontiers emerged. In some cases, the Turks tried to weaken the Allied positions with surprise attacks, while in others, the Allies sought to achieve quick victories to dissuade the Ottomans from continuing the war. While the conflicts involving the Ottomans in the Caucasus, Egypt, and Mesopotamia are not nearly as iconic as the Gallipoli campaign, it is worth taking a look at them to understand the state of the war in the years following its escalation.

When the Ottoman Empire entered the war on the side of the Central Powers, it was hoping to deal blows to the peripheral regions of Russia and the colonial holdings of Britain and France. The Ottomans hoped the Allies would divert a lot of their resources away from the European theaters, where much of the war effort was concentrated.

The fight for the Caucasus served that purpose, with the Ottomans wanting to take Baku, a city that would give them better access to the heart of Britain's possessions in Asia. However, to do that, the Ottomans needed to overcome Russian resistance and fight through Russian-controlled Armenia, which had been heavily fortified since 1878.

The Russians would be the first to engage in November 1914, right as they declared war, advancing toward the Turkish city of Erzurum. The Turkish counteroffensive was launched soon after, with Enver Pasha in command. The Ottoman 3rd Army, counting about 300,000 men in total, was divided into three and ordered to attack the Russian positions separately, something that proved to be a fatal mistake. Initially, the Ottomans took the city of Ardahan but suffered heavy casualties and could not hold onto it for long. They also were decisively defeated in the Battle of Sarikamish, losing more than half of their forces and giving the Russians a much-needed boost in morale.

The Turkish forces suffered from exhaustion and overextension, losing more men to disease and desertion than in battle. By the spring of 1915, it was clear that the Turkish efforts to take Baku would be in vain, and the Ottomans decided to retreat after the Russian offensive in March in Azerbaijan forced them back. What followed were several Russian victories: Erzurum and Trabzon were taken by the end of April, followed by Erzincan in the summer. By that time, the Caucasus was the only region where the Russians had seen massive success, with Tsar Nicholas himself arriving in Armenia in 1915 to show that he would not abandon his Orthodox subjects.

The Armenians preferred living under the rule of Russia instead of Muslim Turkey, and they often sabotaged the

Ottoman forces during the campaign, something that led to the rise of anti-Armenian views in Constantinople. Beginning in early 1915, the Ottomans deported millions of Armenians from their Turkish homes, committing atrocities in the process and killing more than one million innocent civilians. The Armenian genocide would be one of the most horrifying war crimes of World War I. As for the war in the Caucasus, the situation would largely be under Russian control, and no real progress would be made on the front by the Ottomans.

In addition to the Caucasus, fighting also unfolded in Mesopotamia and Egypt, where the British tried to retaliate after the humiliating events of Gallipoli. Before the fight reached Mesopotamia, Britain managed to successfully take the Turkish port city of Basra on the Persian Gulf in November of 1914. Soldiers from the British Raj were organized into an expeditionary force to carry out this operation. With the capture of Basra, Britain assumed a more favorable position and awaited Turkish action.

The activity resumed in December of 1915 when the British tried to force their way to the Turkish city of Kut but abandoned the siege after suffering heavy casualties from the Ottoman defenders for four months. Much of the fighting stopped in Mesopotamia for almost another full year, with only minor skirmishes being carried out in the meantime. For the rest of 1916, the British regrouped and planned an offensive on Baghdad, capturing the city in 1917 with the help of local Arabs who were promised liberation from Ottoman rule. After taking Baghdad, the British in Mesopotamia adopted a more defensive role, instead focusing most of their attention on other fronts in the Middle East.

The situation in Egypt also escalated after the Ottoman Empire's entry into the war. Controlling the Suez Canal and the Red Sea was pivotal to the economic stability of not only Britain but also most of Europe, as every nation relied on trade from Asia, which mostly ran through the canal. The Ottomans directly threatened the safety of the Suez. However, the Ottomans were not aware that the troops who survived Gallipoli would be transported to Egypt to support the Egyptian Expeditionary Force (EEF) in defending the canal. So, the Ottoman efforts to seize the Suez in 1915 and at the beginning of 1916 were largely unsuccessful.

The EEF was more accustomed to fighting in harsh conditions, so they led the Allied forces, who benefited from a newly developed railway system that they used to repel Ottoman attacks. Fighting escalated in August 1916. The British forces of the ANZAC and the EEF were able to defeat a combined Germano-Turkish offensive at the Battle of Romani. Motivated by their success, the British launched a successful counteroffensive to capture the Sinai Peninsula in Palestine, driving out the Ottomans from the area by early 1917.

All of these developments unfolded parallel to each other. Out of the campaigns in which the Ottomans participated, they were only able to find relative success in Gallipoli, but even there, they lost almost 250,000 soldiers. Everywhere else, the superior British and Russian forces were able to easily overcome much of the Ottoman resistance. The Ottoman Empire was plagued with political instability and multiple coups instigated by British intelligence. The Central Powers were left disappointed with the Ottoman Empire's involvement in the war.

Italy Joins the Allies

Italy was perhaps in the most awkward position when the Great War broke out in August 1914. Being a member of the Triple Alliance with Germany and Austria-Hungary, it was bound by the treaty to support its allies in the event of war. However, the treaty stipulated that war had to be declared on them, not the other way around. As you now know, Germany and Austria-Hungary declared war on the Entente, which meant that Italy did not have to side with the Central Powers. The Italians had long been reconsidering their relations with European powers and had never really supported the Triple Alliance in times of crises on the international stage, something that was clearly demonstrated when Italy took the side of France during the First Moroccan Crisis instead of Germany.

Italy had the smallest and the least experienced army out of all the major war participants, so it had to be careful when it came to choosing its role in the conflict. In fact, Italy pursued neutrality for all of 1914. However, as it became clear that neither side had an advantage after the first few months and the countries realized that the war was going to drag on, both sides considered asking the Italians for help. Finally, in April 1915, Italy signed the secret Treaty of London with France, Britain, and Russia, in which the Allies offered Rome the Austro-Hungarian-held provinces that were mainly populated by ethnic Italians, including Trentino, Trieste, South Tirol, Istria, Gorizia, and northern Dalmatia.

This was an offer Rome could not refuse, especially considering the fact that Italy, much like every other nation in 1914, was swept by nationalist sentiment. The people wanted to see a strong and prosperous nation, and the best way to demonstrate Italian might was to "reclaim" the lost territories. Thus, in late May 1915, Italy joined the Allies by declaring war on Austria-Hungary and then on Germany fifteen months later.

The Italian military's inferiority showed when they launched an offensive on the Austrian positions at the Isonzo River in northeastern Italy. Italian commander General Luigi Cadorna wanted to break through modern-day Slovenia but was met with fierce Austrian resistance. Cadorna was also urged to act by the Allies, whose main strategy envisioned the creation of new frontiers since the Western Front had come to a complete standstill.

The Allies were hoping to achieve new breakthroughs against the Central Powers, and the Isonzo and the Gallipoli campaigns held that objective. However, the Austro-Hungarians, perhaps due to the fact that the Italian front was closer to the heart of the empire, did not give the attackers an inch for most of 1915. In what has come to be known as the Battles of the Isonzo, the Italians under Cadorna tried to seize the Austrian positions on twelve different occasions.

Italian troops at the Isonzo River.
https://commons.wikimedia.org/wiki/File:Italian_troops_at_Isonzo_river.jpg

Much like Gallipoli, the region was surrounded by hills, and the troops could only maneuver through the narrow valleys of the Isonzo. This naturally gave the defenders a huge advantage, as they would have more time to set up defenses. The imperial forces would often willingly retreat to the hills to reposition and gain a better defensive foothold. Of the initial five Italian assaults, all of them were repelled successfully by the Austrians by December 1915, with Cadorna losing more than 250,000 men in the process.

The Austrians then launched their own counteroffensive in May of 1916, motivated by the Italians' failure to make progress. They attacked from the Trentino region, which bordered the Alps, and threatened to cut off the rest of the Italian forces at Isonzo if they gained headway. Realizing the danger, General Cadorna recalled the Isonzo offensive and diverted the forces to drive out the Austrians in the north. By late July, the Italians had managed to recover some territory that had been lost to the imperial forces but had still not seen significant results.

New Developments in the Balkan Theater

As we already mentioned, the Ottoman Empire and Bulgaria signed a mutual defensive alliance when the war broke out. And while the Ottomans were being lobbied by the Germans to join World War I on the side of the Central Powers, so were the Bulgarians. Bulgaria, which had been somewhat isolated since its defeat in the Second Balkan War, was in a pretty precarious position and wanted to get revenge on Serbia. The obvious threat that existed with Bulgaria's entry into the war was a potential Russian invasion, which would have been almost impossible to handle. There was also a threat of a united counteroffensive by Serbia and Montenegro. Still, the Bulgarians were easily persuaded to join the Central Powers, which promised to reclaim some of Bulgaria's lost territories. Despite being the smallest Central Power, Bulgaria played a pivotal role due to its active involvement in the Balkan theater. It greatly contributed to Serbia's defeat and provided the Central Powers with a crucial overland route that connected the Ottoman Empire to the rest of Central Europe.

Bulgaria's entry into the war followed a catastrophic Austro-Hungarian invasion of Serbia. By the end of 1914, the imperial army had not gained much progress against the Serbians, who were being supplied by the Allies to hold up the Austrian forces. In early 1915, soon after Serbia reclaimed Belgrade and drove out the enemy forces, the Austrian war effort would mostly be concentrated on the Eastern Front against Russia and at the Isonzo against the Italians. Austria-Hungary requested help from the Germans, who were becoming increasingly annoyed and frustrated by the constant failures of the Austrian army and its inability to perform. Germany sent reinforcements in September of 1915 to renew the invasion of Serbia and make sure that it went smoothly. And to make matters worse for the Serbians, Bulgaria formally declared war in October. By mid-October, Serbia was sandwiched from the north by the Austrians and Germans and in the east and southeast by the Bulgarians.

Bulgaria provided an additional 600,000 troops to the war effort, and it was clear that Serbia did not stand a chance. Thus, in late 1915, the Serbians organized an all-out retreat, hoping to receive at least some assistance from the Allies. After reaching the Adriatic, the Serbs suffered several defeats against the combined forces of the Central Powers, and their Montenegrin allies fell to the invasion. The Serbs were forced to flee to Greece by sea.

The Allies had not expected the war to escalate so quickly in the Balkans. Having just devoted a lot of men to the campaign at Gallipoli, they decided to send a relief force from the amphibious operation to help the Serbs retaliate. The Allied forces, under the command of French General Maurice Sarrail, arrived at the Greek city of Salonica (modern Thessalonica) in early October with the intention of getting to the Serbian border. However, the reinforcements were delayed since King Constantine I had pro-German sentiments. He dismissed the pro-Allied government and did not allow the expeditionary forces to advance any farther.

The situation escalated to the point where the Allied forces effectively took part in the Greek political revolution to install a favorable ruler. They were held up in Salonica until the spring of 1916. Eventually, the Allies managed to defeat the royalist resistance and force King Constantine I to abdicate. By that time, the Serbian positions had been completely overrun by the German-led invasion from the north and the Bulgarian armies from the east, complicating the situation even more.

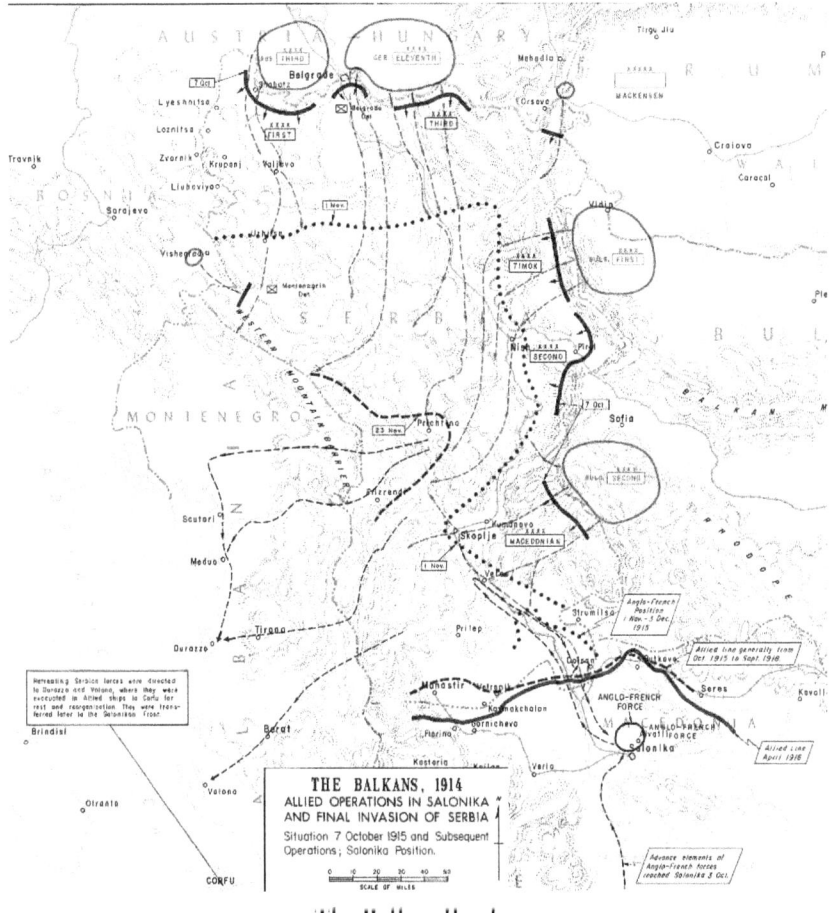

The Balkan theater.

https://commons.wikimedia.org/wiki/File:Serbia-WW1-3.jpg

The Balkan theater would not see any more significant actions for more than a year. By 1916, the Central Powers had managed to defeat Serbia, destroying much of its army and driving them out past their border. Bulgaria occupied the territories that it had wished to regain in the war, but this, paired with the fact that Romania joined the war in mid-1916 on the side of the Allies, complicated matters for the Bulgarian public and the high command. The Bulgarians had achieved their initial goals, but since they had been dragged into an all-out war where the interests of multiple nations had to be taken into consideration, they could not simply abandon the war effort. Forced by the Germans and Austrians to keep up the pressure against their enemies, Bulgaria stayed in the war for longer than it should have, suffering about 300,000 casualties in total—the most losses per capita out of any participating nation.

As for the Allies, after the successful Greek coup, they decided to launch a counteroffensive into Serbia and Macedonia while reinforcing their armies that were stationed in Greece. However, despite seeing some success against the Bulgarians with the Monastir Offensive, the Allies suffered many casualties without being able to achieve meaningful progress. The war effort had been thwarted in the Balkans. And since Serbia had been taken out, the war there favored the Central Powers. By 1917, when Greece formally joined World War I on the side of the Allies, almost 500,000 French, British, Serbian, and Russian troops were being held up in Greece, unable to break through the resistance.

Chapter Ten – The Years of Stalemate

By 1915, both sides had seen an increase in their allies, with the Central Powers being joined by the Ottoman Empire and Bulgaria and the Allies getting Italy. As these new actors became involved in the conflict, it became clear that they provided new opportunities for exploitation. Each side tried to shift the conflict from the heart of Europe to other regions to weaken the enemy.

Since the war developed differently in the new theaters and did not really amount to a decisive swing in the overall balance of power, it is a good time to take a look at what was happening on the Western and Eastern Fronts from early 1915 to 1916. This chapter will focus on the Allied efforts of breaking the stalemate on the Western Front, as well as more exciting developments on the Eastern Front, where Russia was confronted by a new challenger.

Allies Fail on the Western Front

The 740-kilometer (460-mile) front, which was established after the defeat of Germany in the Battle of the Marne, resulted in a complete deadlock for both sides. After entrenching in late summer/early autumn of 1914, no advance whatsoever was made by either the Allies or the Germans, nor was it really possible to break through. The Germans were the first to realize that trench warfare meant a stalemate on the Western Front. As time went by, they started to shift more and more troops to the Eastern Front to help the Austrians against Russia. It was as if Germany was acting according to the intended tactics of the Schlieffen Plan. The nature of trench warfare made it clear that not a lot of soldiers were actually needed to defend a potential Allied advance. Instead, the German high command decided to play the long game by developing its trench systems and making sure that resources were allocated properly to other regions at war.

Chief of staff Moltke was replaced in September of 1914 by Erich von Falkenhayn, who pushed for a defensive strategy in the West and is partially responsible for the almost two-year stalemate in the trenches. By constantly sending supplies to soldiers in the trenches to ensure they would never be overwhelmed by an Allied offensive and even building a whole new "vertical" railway network to better connect the entrenched troops, Germany was in a good position to divert its efforts to the East.

The Allies had a completely different approach. They were eager to break through the German defenses and achieve at least some progress against the Central Powers. The Allied efforts to open up new frontiers served that purpose, as they hoped to pressure their enemies in different regions around the world to indirectly weaken the German defenses in the Western trenches. A coordinated offensive on the weakened Western Front would be the shortest way to the German heartland and, thus, to a victory.

For most of 1915, the Allies tried time and time again to rout the Germans on the Western Front, but the defensive capabilities of the trenches proved too difficult to overcome. The French were especially eager to keep trying to force the breakthrough but met with no success. The Allied high command even considered landing on the German Baltic coast to force the battle to shift away from the trenches, but the strategy was scrapped in favor of renewed efforts on the Western Front.

The constant Allied efforts to storm the German positions on the Western Front proved extremely ineffective, resulting in the loss of about fifty thousand Allied soldiers by early 1915. The high command incorrectly believed that the best way to deal with the enemy's defenses was to continually bombard them with artillery, but the shelling would never happen with a time window that would allow the Allied troops to approach within fighting distance. The German machine guns, which were unstartled by the artillery fire, relentlessly mowed down anyone who tried to cross "no man's land."

Desperate times called for desperate measures. In the late spring of 1915, the Allies launched a major offensive that became known as the Battle of Aubers. The objective was to capture the important Aubers Ridge from the Germans, and the French 10th Army and the BEF (British Expeditionary Forces) tried to break through the front line at three different points. However, their efforts were all in vain. The British forces were completely wiped out, and the French continued their assault until they were forced to retreat back to the trenches in June.

In late September, another combined Allied effort occurred, which also yielded no results and ended in terrible losses, despite unrelenting shelling of German positions. These bombardments, which were intended to weaken and disorient the enemy before the troops were ordered to cross no man's land, actually signaled to the Germans that an assault was imminent, giving them time to call up their reserves and reinforce the bombarded areas. This was the only tactic the Allies used to try and break through the trenches in 1915, and in the end, it resulted in the loss of more than 250,000 French and British lives. The Germans, on the other hand, only lost about half of that amount by the end of the year.

These unsuccessful Allied attempts also had an impact on the British and French economies, with both countries effectively running out of artillery ammunition by the end of 1915. It was clear to the Allies that a continued assault on the trenches would be very costly, and it prompted them to come up with new strategies to circumvent the deadlock. During this time, the war effort against the Ottoman Empire took its real shape, with the Allies sending more troops against the Turks to achieve at least some success in the war. As it stood, they had only suffered losses, and the public back home was growing increasingly weary.

The Great Russian Retreat

Unlike the deadlock on the Western Front, the engagements in the East proved to be much more consequential. After finally taking Przemyśl after months of siege warfare, the Russian troops made significant advances in Galicia, especially when compared to their efforts in East Prussia. The defeat of the Russian armies in the north by the Germans prompted the Russians to devise a plan that strengthened their northern flank while also pushing for the German region of Silesia farther in the west.

The situation was even more complicated for the Central Powers since Austria-Hungary was getting picked on from different sides by different enemies. As a consequence, by mid-1915, the empire had to split its forces to fight off the Serbians and Italians on two fronts while diverting a significant part of its armies to hold off the Russian advance. Although Germany had hoped that Austria-Hungary would be able to stall the Russians for as long as possible, the Austrian army never managed to achieve significant success on its own. Fortunately for Vienna, the stalemate on the Western Front allowed the Germans to shift their focus back to the East more quickly. Throughout 1915, more and more German troops arrived in Galicia to push back the Russians.

Thus, the Central Powers slowly started to consolidate their efforts. In one of the first encounters of 1915, the Germans were able to defeat the Russians in the Second Battle of the Masurian Lakes, dissuading Russian efforts from reinforcing the northern flank. This success prompted the Central Powers to devise a plan that envisioned a concentrated thrust through the Russian center, grouping up the available Austrian and German divisions to overwhelm the opposition. The Gorlice-Tarnów Offensive proved to be extremely successful, with the Central Powers achieving every major objective and pushing the Russians back about eighty miles by June. They even managed to take back control of the lost city of Lemberg and the newly captured Przemyśl.

However, the offensive was perhaps too successful, as the high command of Austria and Germany had not foreseen such progress before the launch of the attack. As a result, they delayed further orders to the troops and gave Russia an opportunity to fully withdraw from the center without suffering more casualties.

The Great Russian Retreat, 1915.
https://commons.wikimedia.org/w/index.php?curid=726155)

As a result of the offensive, the Central Powers had effectively advanced through the very center of the Russian front lines, and Chief of Staff Falkenhayn realized that he needed to seize the opportunity to fully surround the Russian forces on the northern flank, which the Germans and the Austrians had bypassed. The new plan was carried out in July of 1915 and envisioned cutting off the Russian troops that had been stationed in the Warsaw area. However, despite capturing thousands of enemies in the northward offensive from Galicia to southern East Prussia, the Central Powers were not fully able to capitalize. To shorten the time it would take to get to Warsaw, they chose a shorter path rather than enveloping and circling the Russians more from the east. This, in theory, would have made it possible for them to surround even more Russian forces.

The Russians realized the danger they were in and ordered an all-out retreat from the area, giving up whatever progress they had made in the opening months of the war. The Great Retreat saved the lives of many Allied soldiers and allowed Russia to continue the war effort. Still, in total, the tsar's armies lost an estimated 750,000 troops in the span of five months, more than any other European power.

Verdun and the Somme

Parallel to the events on the Eastern Front in 1915, the Allies on the Western Front had largely been recovering from their failed assaults on the German trenches. As we already discussed, these attacks produced a shell shortage in Britain, in addition to costing hundreds of thousands of lives. Thus, for the remainder of 1915, the Allies came up with new plans to achieve success on the Western Front. After the failures of early 1915, Britain and France started conscripting more men, quickly replenishing their losses and preparing for a renewed offensive.

The German high command believed that the war had so far gone very favorably for them. With German reinforcements arriving in Serbia and Russian Poland, as well as the Austro-Hungarians managing to hold off the Italians, Chief of Staff Falkenhayn was confident that a slow approach would be best on the Western Front. Falkenhayn devised a plan that mainly envisioned dealing a significant blow to the Allied positions in the West through an assault on the town of Verdun, which lay in the salient (a narrow breakthrough in the enemy's front lines), favoring a German convergence. Falkenhayn believed that concentrated limited advances onto Verdun would prompt the French to send reserves to defend their positions, drawing out large numbers of enemy soldiers and exposing them to heavy German artillery fire. The French would be compelled to defend Verdun because of its strategic importance and, in the process, suffer a lot of casualties. In fact, Falkenhayn intended to make the French bleed as much as possible to hinder the Allies from launching yet another offensive that would hold up more Germans in the West.

The German troops went on the offensive on February 21st, 1916, bombarding the French positions and setting up for a full-frontal assault. The Meuse River, which ran through the town of Verdun, was crucial, and one of the Germans' initial goals was to successfully take hold of both banks of the river. The first German push was successful, capturing nearby Fort Douaumont after just three days of fighting. The French, realizing that losing Verdun would mean a significant German breakthrough on the Western Front, turned to their allies, urging them to act.

In fact, prior to the German offensive of Verdun, the Allies had all met up in the French town of Chantilly to discuss a united, multi-pronged offensive on the Central Powers. As the fighting at Verdun had escalated, they felt compelled to attack at different points to try and relieve some of the pressure on France. The Italians resumed their offensive at the Isonzo, the Russians tried to break through in the East, and the British replaced the French at Arras on the Western Front, freeing up French troops to be used in Verdun's defense.

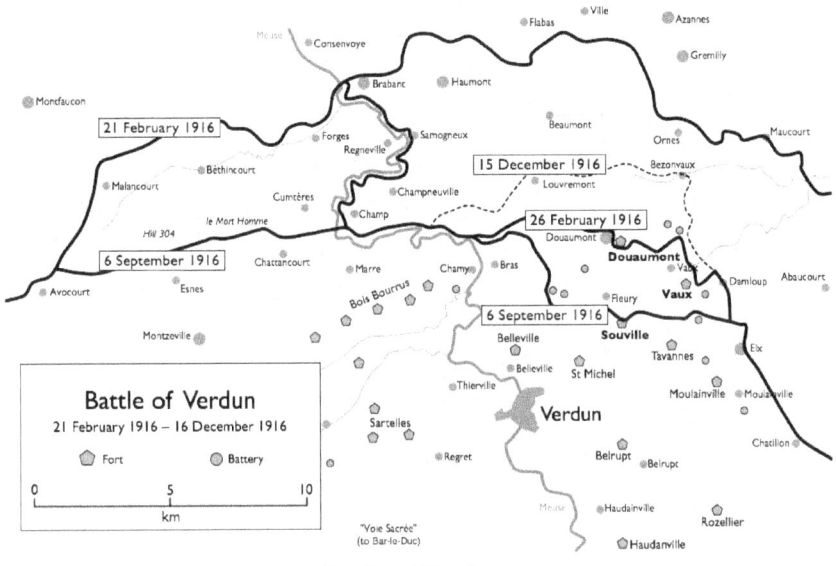

Battle of Verdun.

Drawn by Gdr, CC BY-SA 3.0 <http://creativecommons.org/licenses/by-sa/3.0/>, via Wikimedia Commons. Accessed from: https://commons.wikimedia.org/wiki/File:Battle_of_Verdun_map.png

Still, it was not enough to stop the Germans from advancing. Crucially, French General Phillipe Pétain refused to give up the defensive positions assumed by his forces, ordering fierce counterattacks on the advancing Germans, halting them. The counterattacks bought enough time for the French artillery to mobilize and significantly fire back by mid-March. The outnumbered French were slowly being pushed back, giving up forts along the way for the Germans to occupy and use as defenses. A month later, after the Germans had transferred even more men to reinforce the offensive at Verdun, they began to push even harder, switching from relying on artillery to relying on sheer numbers to break through and force the town to surrender. Eventually, by early June, after about four months of relentless fighting, the Germans came close to capturing the town of Verdun and defeating the French forces. But new developments on the Western Front forced them to delay their advance.

Having agreed to launch a counteroffensive against the Germans and relieve the French defenders at Verdun, the British and French came up with a plan for a concentrated assault in northern France at the Somme River. The Allies finally proceeded with a frontal attack on July 1st, 1916, after a week of heavy bombardment. The Allied offensive at the Somme dissuaded the Germans from sending more reinforcements to the Battle of Verdun, buying much-needed time for the French to retaliate.

Led by British Commander in Chief Douglas Haig, the first efforts to break through the German defenses at the Somme ended disastrously for the BEF 4th Army. The British were ordered to cross a couple of miles of no man's land. Burdened with heavy equipment and confronted with heavy German machine gun fire, the British lost about sixty thousand soldiers in the assault, the most suffered by the Royal Army in a single day. Despite this, General Haig firmly believed that the breakthrough at the Somme was the only way to save the French from being fully defeated at Verdun. After the failure of the first assault, he ordered another attack on the southern part of the German defenses.

Adopting a slower method proved to be more effective, as the Brits managed to achieve some success by July 14th by breaking the Germans at Ovillers. Even though Haig was optimistic about further advances, he decided to continue partial assaults on German positions for the next two months. No significant ground was gained, but the British were able to keep a large portion of the German army on the Western Front occupied. In September, the first tanks were used at the Somme, but it amounted to no real success for the British. In the end, the Allies decided to dig in, accepting the fact that further advancement seemed impossible. The British suffered an estimated 400,000 casualties at the Somme. The Battle of the Somme also saw 150,000 French causalities and about 550,000 Germans. By late September, the offensive had been abandoned, having gained no real victory, although it was justified by the fact that it was able to act as a diversion for the German forces at Verdun.

The British offensive at the Somme.
https://commons.wikimedia.org/wiki/File.Going_over_the_top_01.jpg

The Allied counteroffensive at the Somme dramatically influenced the course of the Battle of Verdun, where the French were able to transfer reinforcements and reorganize after the Germans' inactivity throughout the course of the summer. Starting in September, the French, now under the command of General Charles Mangin, retaliated, recapturing the important Douaumont and Vaux forts by December. The French advanced slowly and firmly, while the Germans, who had fewer resources, were forced to give up their gains at Verdun. The fighting largely ceased in mid-December, after which the French troops were able to stabilize the situation and reestablish defensive positions.

All in all, the Battle of Verdun lasted for 302 days, with about 350,000 casualties on each side. It has become one of the most famous battles of World War I, synonymous with bloodshed and French resilience.

The Brusilov Offensive

As two of the most famous battles of WWI unfolded on the Western Front, there was also significant activity on the Eastern Front, where the Russians tried to mount another offensive to weaken Germany and help relieve the pressure on the West. With many Germans occupied by fighting France and Britain and the Austro-Hungarians sending more forces to deal with Italy, the Russian high command believed that it was the right time to strike and recover from the Great Retreat.

Under the leadership of General Alexander Brusilov, Russia devised a plan to attack the Austro-Hungarians in Galicia and reclaim Russian Poland. By the start of the operation on June 4th, 1916, the front line between Russia and the Central Powers had been pushed to the east, stretching southward from the Baltic coast and the city of Riga to the Romanian border. However, in about two months, the Russians had managed to make significant progress and pushed the Austrian and German troops west of Warsaw, marking one of the most impressive offensives on the Eastern Front.

The success of the Brusilov Offensive is attributed to the careful planning that took place months before its launch, with the Russian high command correctly realizing that their forces would face limited Austrian resistance during the assault because of the latter's war with Italy. The four armies under General Brusilov coordinated remarkably well, easily crushing the ill-prepared Austro-Hungarian troops and forcing them to retreat after a series of rapid assaults on their positions. The Austro-Hungarians surrendered in large numbers, with the Russians capturing an estimated 200,000 soldiers at Czernowitz, a number that increased up to 400,000 by the end of the offensive in September. The total number of casualties for the Central Powers amounted to more than a million, with about 90 percent of the losses coming from the Austro-Hungarians. The Brusilov offensive was a remarkable victory that demonstrated the true military strength of Russia.

However, despite forcing the Austro-Hungarians all the way back to the Carpathian Mountains, the Brusilov Offensive did not end in the way the Russian high command had hoped for. The constant shortage of supplies and lack of proper communications were a massive problem for the Russians, who, after the arrival of the Germans, were forced to retreat, afraid that the salient they had established could be flanked by the German forces. In addition, Brusilov's advances came at a massive cost. There were an estimated one million Russian casualties, most of them being captured or deserted. General Brusilov was disappointed by the lack of discipline, which undermined his efforts to continue pressuring the Central Powers. The Brusilov Offensive was perhaps the final positive thing that would happen to Russia for the rest of the war.

A direct consequence of Russia's success in the offensive was Romania's entry into the war on the side of the Allies in August 1916. The Allies promised Romania the Austrian province of Transylvania, which had historically been a part of Romania and was largely inhabited by Romanians. However, Romania's entry into the war did not produce the results the Allies had hoped for. After a relatively slow offensive in Transylvania by the Romanian military, the Central Powers were quick to respond by organizing a counteroffensive from Bulgaria that easily thrust into southern Romania. The Bulgarians, with German reinforcements and under German command, quickly pushed their way through the Romanian defenses, achieving victory after victory until eventually reaching Bucharest in December. The Romanian capital fell on December 6th, 1917, and the army was forced to retreat north into Moldova and seek shelter under Russian protection.

Chapter Eleven - The War at Sea

Having covered the most significant military developments since the start of the war up until late 1916, it is time to look at a crucial part of World War I—the war at sea. We briefly touched upon the naval side of the conflict when we discussed the Ottoman Empire's "purchase" of two German warships, the *Goeben* and the *Breslau*, something that was one of the precursors to the Ottomans' entry into the war on the side of the Central Powers. However, this was only a small part of the naval developments that took place during the Great War. This chapter will focus on the crucial events that shaped the naval war between the two sides, focusing on the rivalry between Britain and Germany that escalated to an all-out conflict at sea and revolutionized warfare.

The Early Encounters

Before the beginning of the war, Germany made significant efforts to try and catch up with Britain in terms of naval strength. By the end of the 19th century, it was increasingly believed that possessing a strong navy was the key to global domination. Britain had enjoyed naval supremacy for centuries, possessing the largest fleet out of all the major powers and having experienced and disciplined personnel. Still, Germany managed to make up the disparity that existed with Britain by the start of the war. Despite not outnumbering the Royal Navy, the Germans were confident they could hold their own against the British.

The dreadnoughts dominated the naval arsenals of both nations. The ships were armed with several large and small guns and reinforced with steel to give them durability. Throughout the course of the war, naval technology developed drastically, with the creation and increased use of battlecruisers, torpedo boats, and submarines. Battlecruisers were basically modified versions of the dreadnoughts, with some lacking armor for greater speed and others housing more artillery for power. Torpedo boats, also known as destroyers, were smaller ships that were very quick and effective in rapid encounters. The submarines, which became very prominent with the German U-boats, were not as good at fighting warships but were extremely effective at pressuring naval blockades and carrying out surprise attacks.

German U-boat with its crew.

https://commons.wikimedia.org/wiki/File:German_U-boat_UB_14_with_its_crew.jpg

The first major battle between the Germans and Brits on the high seas was the Battle of the Helgoland Bight in late August of 1914. A part of the British fleet managed to destroy several German light cruisers and kill about one thousand men while only suffering thirty-five casualties in return. The Germans retaliated, thanks to their submarines, which were still a fresh invention at the beginning of the war. Throughout October, the German U-boats proved to be problematic, as they were scattered in the North Sea, dealing significant blows to several British warships. Still, in the encounters on the ocean, the Brits were able to defeat parts of the German High Seas Fleet. In January of 1915, at the Battle of Dogger Bank, the German cruiser *Blücher* was sunk by the Royal Navy without suffering any casualties.

Where the Germans saw more success at sea were in other parts of the world, especially in East Asia, where the German High Seas Fleet held a squadron of four battlecruisers under Admiral Graf Maximilian von Spee. Through quick and concentrated bombardments, the squadron created a lot of problems for the British, who had to keep an eye on their vast possessions in Asia and Oceania, stretching their navy thin to defend different locations. In addition to damaging Allied trade, the Germans also sailed to the shores of British and French possessions, where they shelled the ports that were used to transport Allied colonial troops to the front lines in Europe. The German cruiser *Emden*, for example, was able to destroy up to fifteen Allied transport ships on its own by November of 1914 until finally being sunk off the Cocos Islands by the Royal Navy.

The rest of the squadron was reinforced by Germany by the end of the month, and it achieved an impressive victory against the British ships in the Battle of Coronel, where it sunk two British cruisers without losing any of theirs. To deal with the German East Asian squadron, Britain sent more ships to the Pacific and Indian Oceans. The Royal Navy was able to finally catch the Germans near the Pacific South American coast. Under Admiral Sir Doveton Sturdee, eight British cruisers chased down the German squadron and sank all of the enemy ships. Through this victory, they put a much-needed end to the disturbance of trade that had been caused by Germany.

Blockades

Since both sides realized they could significantly damage each other's economies by interfering with international trade and the colonies, Germany and Britain viciously engaged to dominate the transporting corridors and cut off each other's supply lines. Right at the beginning of the war, Britain organized a huge naval blockade of Germany by covering the two points at sea the Germans used to access international trade: the English Channel and the entry to the

North Sea off the coast of Scotland. Covering the narrower Strait of Dover with sea mines was enough to dissuade the German ships from taking that route. In the north, the Royal Navy deployed a squadron of heavy and light cruisers to patrol a large area and make sure that no material that could be used for the war reached the German coast.

To answer the blockade, Germany began relying on its submarines, which proved to be extremely effective at taking out merchant ships. In fact, partly due to the fact that the German East Asian surface squadron had been destroyed by the Royal Navy, the Germans upped their production and usage of U-boats. By early 1915, submarine attacks were carried out on non-military ships only after the Germans issued warnings to the target ships to ensure the safe evacuation of innocent crews. However, as time went by, the Allies adapted and began dealing with the U-boats by implementing new defense measures like underwater nets, new types of mines, special depth bombs to target the submarines, and new radars that were capable of detecting sound waves generated from the rustling German engines underwater. The Allies also started arming and reinforcing their merchant ships to avoid too much damage. France also helped out significantly, as it fielded a decent navy to support Britain. Together, the Allies managed to overcome the submarine problem.

The situation did not get better for Germany throughout 1915, as the Germans declared the waters near the British Isles were hostile, claiming that they were entitled to attack any ship, Allied or not, as they deemed necessary. The neutral countries did not welcome this decision, correctly believing that Germany had no right to open fire on ships that had nothing to do with the war and were just conducting regular activities. The public's discontent toward Germany reached its peak in May 1915 when the German submarines sunk the British liner *Lusitania*, which was one of the biggest transport ships in the world. It was on its way to Liverpool from New York. Over a thousand innocent civilians died, including 128 US citizens.

The international community, especially the United States, adopted an increasingly anti-German stance after this event, but the US government, staying in line with its neutrality policy, calmed public sentiment, which was clamoring for war with Germany. The Germans would provoke the US on several more occasions by sinking other non-military ships. The United States' protests would eventually lead to Germany ceasing all of its submarine activity west of the British Isles in late 1915.

RMS Lusitania in 1907.
https://commons.wikimedia.org/wiki/File:Lusitania_1907.jpg

Jutland

The most important and most famous development of the naval war would unfold in May 1916. The newly appointed commander in chief of the German High Seas Fleet, Admiral Reinhard Scheer, carefully observed the British Royal Navy's movements in early 1916, believing the Germans had an opportunity to exploit a temporary numerical superiority and deal a massive blow to the British. With the main part of the Royal Navy patrolling near the Orkney Islands, Admiral Scheer devised a plan that envisioned engaging with the British fleet on the English east coast. Scheer believed the Germans would be able to effectively overcome the British Royal Navy's strength and achieve a decisive victory.

Fortunately for the Allies, British intelligence was able to intercept and decode a part of the transmission from the German high command and immediately alerted Admiral John Jellicoe, who was in charge of the Grand Fleet, to reinforce Admiral David Beatty and his men. The Germans were still quick to attack Beatty's ships, overwhelming them with firepower and sinking one cruiser. After most of Beatty's ships were mobilized and returning fire, the Germans sent out their destroyers with a torpedo attack, sinking another battleship, the *Queen Mary*.

Admiral Beatty realized he could not hold the German fleet any longer and decided to retreat northward to stall for time until Admiral Jellicoe arrived. For the next hour, the Germans pursued Beatty's ships, which led them to Jellicoe's squadron that had set up a battle line, ready for the enemy to arrive. For the next half an hour, the Germans maneuvered through a barrage from the British Royal Navy, only managing to reorganize thanks to the durability of their ships and the discipline of the crew. They were able to return fire quickly.

Then, in an extraordinary turn of events, Admiral Scheer, realizing that his ships were still facing an organized battle line, ordered the Germans to carry out a 180-degree turn to avoid a full confrontation with the British. This was an extremely risky and difficult maneuver for one ship, let alone a whole array of massive cruisers and battleships, but it was executed perfectly by the experienced and well-trained German crew.

Scheer directed his ships south, and Admiral Jellicoe ordered his fleet to chase down the Germans in a parallel line from the east, leading the two sides to fire heavily on each other's positions. By 7 p.m., both sides had suffered significant casualties, and it became clear to Admiral Scheer that the Royal Navy's position blocked the German ships from the German coast, meaning the British had cut off their potential escape path.

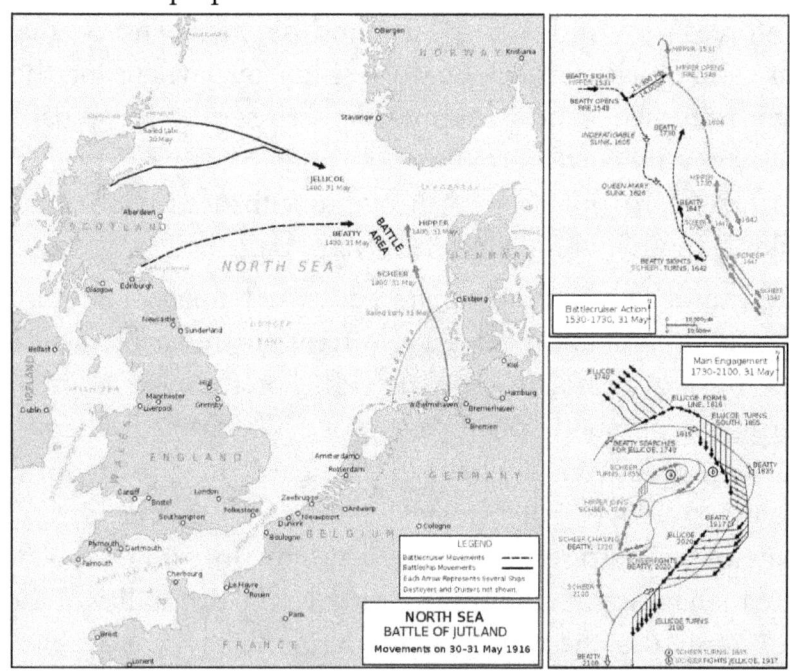

Battle of Jutland.

Grandiose, CC BY-SA 3.0 <https://creativecommons.org/licenses/by-sa/3.0>, via Wikimedia Commons. Accessed from: https://commons.wikimedia.org/wiki/File:Map_of_the_Battle_of_Jutland,_1916.svg

In a last desperate move to break the British, Scheer ordered a full-frontal charge with his cruisers, a move that was unheard of because it gave a massive advantage to the British, who could calmly fire on the approaching Germans. However, since Admiral Jellicoe had also seen a lot of damage, he was afraid the Germans might overwhelm his fleet. He ordered the Royal Navy to turn back and sail away from the charge. If Jellicoe had correctly weighed the danger posed to his positions by the German forces, he would have stood his ground and completely destroyed the Germans. But after hours of fighting and in total darkness, it was difficult to assume what the Germans were capable of, and Admiral Jellicoe acted accordingly, saving what was left of his forces.

The Battle of Jutland was the biggest naval battle in history up until that point. At the end of the battle, both sides claimed victory, while, in reality, the results were indecisive. The Germans had managed to inflict more losses on the British but could not capitalize and effectively carry out their intended objectives. In the end, despite the losses suffered by the British, the Germans were not able to undermine the Royal Navy's strength in the North Sea, as the British ships continued the blockade and still outnumbered the German High Seas Fleet for the rest of the war.

Chapter Twelve – Russia Out, United States In

This chapter will focus on arguably two of the most important non-military developments in World War I: the Russian Revolution and Russia's subsequent exit of the war and the events that caused the United States to enter the war on the side of the Allies. These events significantly turned the tide of the war and affected its final outcome. Although they happened parallel to each other, we will first examine how the mass discontent in Russia resulted in a socialist revolution and then turn our attention to the fatal telegram from Germany that caused the United States to break its neutrality.

The February Revolution

The year 1917 turned out to be a momentous one for Russia. The events of 1917 did not only change the course of the country forever but also had long-lasting consequences that affected the rest of the world for decades to come. Of course, we cannot fully cover the political and social extent of the Russian Revolution; instead, we will be focusing on how Russia's participation in the Great War influenced the events of 1917.

When World War I broke out in 1914, Russia was swept up, much like every other nation, in nationalist fervor. People of all classes demonstrated their firm support for the war effort and were ready to prove their patriotism. Due to this, many overlooked the economic and social hardships the country had been struggling with for the past decades, giving the tsar and his regime hope that the Russian public would adopt a more royalist stance if they achieved success in the war. And they could see some favorable results in this regard when the Russian army achieved victories in Galicia and the Caucasus.

However, by the end of 1916, things were not going well for Russia. After two years, with an estimated five million casualties, the Russian army was losing more and more men after the partially successful Brusilov Offensive. The prolonged war had detrimental effects not only on the morale of the soldiers, who mutinied time and time again and deserted on multiple occasions, but also on the Russian economy, which still had not achieved similar levels of industrialization as other major powers in the war. This meant that Russia could not keep up the war effort on a similar scale and quality as its enemies. And when paired with the government's incompetence in finding solutions during wartime, the people were greatly discontented.

The crisis finally amounted to a series of protests in late February 1917 in St. Petersburg. The public took to the streets, protesting the inadequacy of the tsar's regime, as well as new food rationing laws that had been put in place a couple of days prior. During the next week, the protesters grew in numbers. The government became concerned that the demonstrations could turn into something bigger. At that time, Tsar Nicholas II was not present in St. Petersburg, having arrived at the Caucasian front to personally lead the Russian forces against the Ottomans. This infuriated the protesters even more, who viewed the tsar as a traitor, leaving the struggling people behind in search of some glory in the war.

From February 21st to February 28th, the protests slowly turned into armed confrontations with the city's police, but by the end of the week, even the city's garrison had joined the demonstrators, refusing to execute orders from the high command. Tsar Nicholas was forced to return to the capital after learning of the events that had transpired, but it was all in vain. Nicholas II failed to find enough support and was forced to abdicate three days later on March 3rd, nominating his brother, Grand Duke Michael Alexandrovich, to take his place. His brother declined the offer. This marked the end of the Romanov dynasty. As a result, a provisional government was set up to lead the country during the crisis.

Peace, Land, and Bread

However, this was not the end to Russia's problems, nor to the revolution. The provisional government had no time to address the Russian people's immediate problems, as there was an empty treasury and limited resources. In addition, Russian troops, which had been suffering defeat after defeat and had been ill-supplied for months, lost practically all motivation to fight after having learned of the situation back home. Because of the change in leadership in St. Petersburg, the army's chain of command had been distorted, and the soldiers were confused about what to do. Thousands deserted every week. Still, the provisional government insisted on continuing the war effort and could not implement any substantial changes for the unhappy population. This caused yet another series of mass protests over the course of the summer. The protestors were dealt with violently.

In the wake of all of this, some political organizations recognized the opportunity to influence developments. Among them was the Bolshevik Party, which managed to gain a lot of traction. The Bolshevik Party was a far-left party led by Vladimir Lenin and stressed the necessity of a social revolution and the triumph of the lower-class proletariat over the corrupt bourgeoisie. Motivating the local soviets (civil society groups where people of the lower classes assembled to discuss and assess Russian politics) with their catchy slogan of "peace, land, and bread," the Bolsheviks urged the Russians to revolt. The public was once again swept up in an uproar, supporting Lenin and his movement and bursting out onto the streets once again in October 1917.

These demonstrations were far more brutal, with armed protesters and the police violently clashing for days. In the end, the Bolsheviks triumphed. The demonstrators were able to storm the White Palace in St. Petersburg, arrest the members of the provisional government, and declare Russia as a socialist state led by the Bolsheviks.

The Bolsheviks suddenly gained the authority to rule Russia and influence its domestic and foreign policy decisions. One of the first things the new government did was negotiate a separate peace treaty with the Germans— the Treaty of Brest-Litovsk—which marked the end of Russian involvement in World War I. Prioritizing peace to please the upset public, Lenin and his government approved the Decree on Peace almost right away. Russia and the

Central Powers agreed to an armistice in December.

After two months of negotiations at the German-controlled town of Brest-Litovsk, the two sides, with German, Austro-Hungarian, Bulgarian, Ottoman, and Russian delegations present, agreed to the terms of the peace treaty in early March 1918. Russia was forced to cede control of Lithuania, Latvia, Estonia, Ukraine, Belarus, and Finland, which were most of its European holdings. In addition, it returned the provinces gained from Turkey during the war in 1878, with the three Caucasian nations of Georgia, Armenia, and Azerbaijan declaring their independence and forming the Transcaucasian Democratic Federative Republic. In addition to territorial losses, Russia also promised to pay war reparations to Germany, which would amount to six billion German marks.

Just like that, in the span of two revolutions, Russia was out of the war. It was a massive victory for the Central Powers, as Russia's exit freed up the forces on the Eastern Front. Germany had largely incited the Russian Revolution by allowing Vladimir Lenin, who was in Switzerland in 1917, to pass through its territories to get to St. Petersburg and lead the revolutionary movement. In the end, Russia was left empty-handed, while the Central Powers had clearly gained a big advantage.

However, as we will soon see, the Central Powers were not able to capitalize on the results of the Russian Revolution, as the Allies managed to get a new ally on their side, which upset the balance of power once again.

The Zimmermann Telegram

We have barely mentioned the United States in this book. This is largely due to the fact that American involvement in World War I was not very prominent or impactful for the first two years of the war. The American government pursued isolationism, which had characterized US foreign policy since the early 19th century. In addition, due to the absence of a major imminent threat in North America, the US Army was significantly smaller than its European counterparts, with an estimated 400,000 active personnel compared to, for example, about 4 million British troops. However, the United States still contributed greatly to the Allied war effort, supplying Britain and France with all sorts of goods, including arms and ammunition. Despite this, at the beginning of the war, the US did not exactly view Germany as hostile, having had somewhat of a warm relationship with the Reich since German unification in 1871. The US also had a sizeable German diaspora.

So, the US, led by President Woodrow Wilson, tried to play the role of an intermediary between the Allies and the Central Powers, offering to lead peace negotiations on multiple occasions. At the beginning of the war, peace negotiations were not seen by either side as possible, let alone necessary, since both believed they had the upper hand. But as the war dragged on and millions of people died, the belligerents thought about stopping the war and diplomatically resolving the conflict.

For example, after talks with both sides in December 1916, Wilson proposed a "peace without victory" to the warring nations, something the British side, for the first time since the beginning of the war, viewed as favorable. It is likely that the French would have also been persuaded if the British and Americans had pushed for such a resolution. The Austro-Hungarians likely would have been on board since the war had been the most crushing for the dual monarchy. However, being the first to sue for peace would be regarded as a political defeat and a display of weakness. President Wilson soon discontinued his efforts.

Technically, Germany "wanted" peace, but the terms presented by the Germans in January 1917 were absurd, something akin to the Austrian ultimatums to Serbia back in 1914. Accepting them would have practically meant the ceding of German-occupied France and Belgium to the Reich, something the Allies would have never accepted in the first place.

The situation dramatically changed after Germany decided to conduct unrestricted submarine warfare in January before declaring it to the rest of the world on February 1st. Germany gave itself the ability to interfere and engage with any foreign ship that entered the North Sea while warning countries to evacuate their civilians. It was perhaps an overly confident move from the Reich, as it restricted not only the movement of the Allied ships but also US merchant ships. Two days later, the Americans cut off diplomatic ties with Germany and decided to reinforce and arm all ships that were set to pursue trade with Britain and France. However, despite the unrestricted submarine warfare, the Germans were wise enough not to attack any passing US ships, knowing that it would create anti-German public sentiment in the US and risk war.

Despite this, the German high command made another inconsiderate move that did raise of anti-German sentiment in America. On February 24th, President Woodrow Wilson received a decoded telegram intercepted by British intelligence. The infamous message, which has come to be known as the Zimmermann Telegram, was directed to the newly elected Mexican President Venustiano Carranza by German Foreign Secretary Arthur Zimmermann.

Zimmermann proposed German support to Mexico against the US if the Americans entered the war against Germany, something that was a sound possibility due to the recent rise in tensions between the two countries. In the event of victory, Zimmermann promised Carranza the return of territories Mexico had lost during the Mexican-American War, namely the US states of Arizona, New Mexico, and Texas. To the US, this proposal was a clear sign that Germany was a hostile nation, especially after taking into consideration the fact that the US was not on friendly terms with Mexico either.

After days of consideration, the telegram was published in the press, and the public response that followed was what Germany had feared all along. The whole nation had changed their views regarding the war, with the majority calling for America's entry into the war. Seeing the situation escalate, Mexico promptly declined to engage in any sort of military action against the US, while Germany resorted to increasing its submarine attacks, realizing that it had angered the US beyond the turning point. Throughout March, President Wilson observed the situation unfold and called for a joint session of Congress on April 2nd to discuss America's entry into the war against Germany. In his speech, the president referred to the prospect of US involvement as a highly undesired necessity and stressed that German actions had forced the United States to act decisively.

Four days later, on April 6th, 1917, the United States entered the war on the side of the Allies, although it only declared war on Germany and not all of the Central Powers.

Part Four – The End of the War

Chapter Thirteen – Last Chance for Germany

This chapter will focus on the German Spring Offensive of March 1918 and the events that led up to it, including the Nivelle Offensive on the Western Front. We will analyze these developments and paint a picture of World War I in its final and most decisive year, where an array of misjudgments and surprises greatly influenced the final outcome of the war.

The Allies Fail Again

The entry of the US into the war gave the Allies new hope and the drive to continue the fight, especially on the Western Front. By the time the United States had sent its divisions to France to reinforce the Allied efforts, Britain, France, and Italy all knew that it would only be a matter of time before Russia was forced to surrender or leave the Eastern Front. Thus, the Allies perceived the months following April 1917 as crucial, believing that only a sudden breakthrough of the German positions on the Western Front would ensure their victory. If the Allies did not emerge triumphant, Germany and Austria-Hungary would have the time to transfer their Eastern divisions to the Western Front, reinforcing their defenses and giving the Central Powers numerical superiority.

The plan of attack was drawn up before April by the new commander of the French forces, Robert Nivelle. It envisioned a combined Franco-British breakthrough of the German defenses in Champagne and the capture of the pivotal Chemin des Dames by the French forces, while the British divisions engaged simultaneously at Arras to try and gain the high ground and force the enemy to retreat.

The plan, as always, seemed sound and cohesive; however, just like in the past, officials were overly optimistic and refused to take all variables into consideration. Most importantly, the majority of the French Army was completely exhausted after fighting viciously at Verdun for months. Unlike most of 1915, when the newly entrenched forces rarely went on full-frontal offensives, the soldiers had no time to rest in between defensive and offensive operations. Thus, the Nivelle Offensive was a massive gamble. If the plan did not work as intended, the French soldiers' poor morale could result in disaster.

In the end, the plan was partially successful. It was launched in early April 1917, with the Germans aware of the general objectives of the Allies. The British saw better success at Arras than the French did at the Aisne. The British attack caught the Germans off-guard, inflicting many casualties and forcing them to fall back. In the battle, the Canadian corps heroically achieved victory at Vimy Ridge, which gave the British forces a massive advantage, as they were able to defeat the Germans. The French, on the other hand, despite carrying out the plan to the best of their ability and partially reaching the intended objectives, saw more losses than Nivelle had planned—about 135,000 casualties in total, with 30,000 of them deaths.

By late April, the Allied efforts had been largely successful, but to ensure a decisive victory, non-stop fighting was necessary. On May 3rd, in an unfortunate turn of events for Commander Nivelle, the French 21st Division, which had been ordered to go on the offensive, refused to carry out its orders. The French Army mutinied en masse, with most of the troops refusing to attack because of exhaustion and poor supplies. About twenty thousand soldiers deserted in May.

The Spring Offensive

The rest of 1917 went favorably for the Central Powers. Parallel to the failure of the Allies to achieve success on the Western Front, the Russian Revolution had effectively knocked Russia out of the war by late 1917. The German high command was optimistic. It believed that to ensure victory, Germany just had to hold out on the Western Front for as long as possible, giving the Eastern divisions enough time to join up and launch a final assault on the Allied positions in France. Germany's hopes were especially high after the Allies could not break through the Hindenburg Line, an extremely well-organized line of German defenses. It had been organized by General Paul von Hindenburg himself after the Nivelle Offensive.

Seeing that the bulk of the US forces was still on the way and that the French morale was low, General Erich Ludendorff drew up plans for the offensive, which was supposed to achieve a decisive German victory by splitting up the Allied forces on the Western Front. The Spring Offensive envisioned a rapid assault on the Allied positions while the Germans still had numerical superiority, thanks to their reinforcements from the Eastern Front. The German high command ordered assaults on five different Allied points to separate the enemy.

On March 21st, 1918, Germany started its advance, using a completely new method to overcome the Allied defenses. The new Hutier tactic, named after German General Oskar von Hutier, saw smaller, better-trained groups of troops bypassing the most heavily defended points to achieve victory at weaker points, mainly areas in charge of logistics or communications. After these troops infiltrated the points, the main infantry corps, with the support of artillery fire, would overwhelm the Allied positions. The Hutier tactic was fundamentally different from anything either side had done before, as the forces would focus on weakening enemy defenses with artillery barrages before trying to cross no man's land with everything they had. As it turned out, the tactic was extremely successful. The Allies could not find an effective answer, causing them to suffer many casualties in the first days of fighting. The Germans made significant advances of some forty miles into the Allied positions and started to close in toward Paris.

German artillery during the Spring Offensive.

https://commons.wikimedia.org/wiki/File:The_German_Spring_Offensive,_March-july_1918_Q8629.jpg

However, these quick, smaller-scale assaults meant that it took more time for the bulk of the German forces with their slower-moving artillery to follow and clean up the resistance. Thus, despite their advantageous position, the Germans could not capitalize on their gains and were forced to stop the offensive soon after its launch. After a month of suffering heavy casualties, the Allies started to retaliate, consolidating their forces. They were further motivated to fight after the increased arrival of American troops.

In July 1918, in a desperate effort to finally break through, the Germans started the Second Battle of the Marne, hoping to fully exploit their numerical superiority. But their efforts were thwarted, as they were confronted with reinforcements from the American Expeditionary Forces, which dissuaded them from continuing the attack. Thus, the Spring Offensive, albeit achieving some initial success, was effectively stopped in the summer of 1918. Throughout the campaign, Germany lost about 600,000 men, while the combined casualties of the Allies numbered more than 800,000.

Chapter Fourteen – The Fall of the Central Powers

The Spring Offensive was the final major attempt from the Central Powers to achieve a decisive victory and break the Allies. Since the offensive's intended objectives were not reached, the Allies realized that the momentum had swung back into their favor on the Western Front with the arrival of the AEF (American Expeditionary Forces). Thus, the Allies struck simultaneously both on the Western Front and on the Ottoman front in one of the largest campaigns of World War I. The Hundred Days Offensive produced remarkable results and eventually led to the Allied victory in the war.

The Fall of the Ottomans

The fighting between the Allies and the Ottomans never ceased, unlike what transpired in Europe. Because of the Ottoman Empire's massive size, the Allies were able to strike at different locations, stretching the Turkish forces thin and limiting their resources and cohesiveness. Over time, due to constant clashes with the Allies, who were getting reinforcements from their colonial territories, the

Ottoman army became exhausted. The main leverage the Ottomans had over the Allies was their numerical superiority, but they were far less technologically advanced or disciplined than the British or the French. Their poor discipline showed as the fighting continued. After suffering humiliating defeats during the Gallipoli campaign, the Allies retaliated and broke the Ottoman Empire.

The Allies saw the most success in the Sinai and Palestine campaign, which lasted for over three years, from early 1915 to mid-1918. Over the course of the campaign, the Egyptian Expeditionary Forces (EEF) achieved victory after victory, fighting their way through the Palestinian lands after suffering some setbacks in the First and Second Battles of Gaza in the spring of 1917. The British then achieved a victory at the crucial Battle of Mughar Ridge in November 1917, as they were able to break out of the stalemate that had ensued after their defeats at Gaza. Seeing the low morale of the Ottoman troops, they pushed northward, capturing the city of Jerusalem in December. Taking control of Jerusalem, which held immense symbolic importance, was a reassuring moment for the Allies and a precursor to their following success.

In early 1918, to reinforce the Western Front against the German Spring Offensive, many of the EEF soldiers were sent right from the Ottoman front lines, causing the Allied efforts to slow down for a little bit. However, thanks to Britain's immense colonial holdings, it was able to swiftly transfer Indian corps to fill the ranks of the EEF and dissuade the Ottomans from launching a counteroffensive. After retraining and resting its soldiers in the summer, the British high command began organizing a new plan of attack to break the bulk of the Ottoman defenses at Palestine and push them back to Anatolia. In September, the Allies proceeded with their operations, crushing the Ottomans at the crucial Battle of Megiddo. Only six thousand of thirty-five thousand Turkish soldiers escaped capture.

The victory at Megiddo was followed by another series of Allied victories. In the ensuing battles of Tulkarm and Nablus, the Ottomans lost their military headquarters and, thus, much of their ability to continue an effective war effort in the Middle East. The Allies closed in from all directions, seeing success in Mesopotamia and the Transjordan. One of the final decisive moments of the Sinai and Palestine campaign was the capture of Damascus on September 30th, 1918, by the British XXI Corps and the Desert Mounted Corps. With Damascus and all of the Middle East under British control and the Allies slowly converging on Anatolia and threatening Istanbul from the Balkans, the Ottomans realized they had lost the war.

The Ottoman Empire's defeat was finalized with the signing of the Armistice of Mudros on October 30th, 1918. Since the war had unfolded unfavorably throughout all of 1918, the Ottoman government hid the news of their defeats back home to not incite an already upset public, which had been massively affected by the war. Ottoman Grand Vizier Talaat Pasha visited Germany and Bulgaria in September to personally inquire about the Central Powers' plans to continue fighting but left empty-handed. With no hope left, Talaat Pasha resigned from office in late October, urging the other members of the government to follow his example since he believed the Allies would punish them for conducting the war. Three days after his resignation, Ahmed Izzet Pasha, who replaced Talaat as the grand vizier, signed an armistice with the British Admiral Somerset Arthur

Gough-Calthorpe on board the British HMS *Agamemnon*.

From the very beginning, the Ottoman entry into the war was a big gamble, based on the hopes of achieving quick victories and motivated by the public's irredentist sentiments. In reality, the Ottoman Empire was in no shape to contest the European powers, as it lagged behind them in all aspects, which clearly showed over the course of their time in the war. The Armistice of Mudros brought about the Ottoman Empire's end. The Ottomans removed their soldiers from all locations, including the Caucasus, the Middle East, and the Balkans, and surrendered to the Allies, who assumed control of Ottoman Anatolia and briefly occupied Istanbul before the end of the war. The armistice was later followed by the Treaty of Sèvres, which had even more detrimental effects on the Ottomans.

The Sinai and Palestine campaign was a historic demonstration of the British colonial forces acting together as one. The cooperation between the Egyptian, Indian, Australian, New Zealand, and Canadian troops brought victory to Britain and the Allies. Back in Britain, the public was largely unaware of the campaign's significance, as most of their attention was on the Western Front. However, the true scope and importance of the campaign were quickly realized by the British government, which praised the colonial troops for their bravery and contribution to the war effort.

The Hundred Days Offensive

Meanwhile, the situation was getting tense on the Western Front, where the Allies had finally welcomed the bulk of the American Expeditionary Forces and had high hopes to once and for all end the war. What ensued in the late summer of 1918 has come to be known as the Hundred

Days Offensive, which was perhaps the most important campaign in World War I. Devised by Allied Supreme Commander in Chief Ferdinand Foch of France, it envisioned taking matters back into Allied hands after the failed German Spring Offensive and breaking through the infamous Hindenburg Line, which was heavily defended by the Germans.

Thus, the Allies got to work, initiating the Battle of Amiens on August 8th, 1918. In the battle, the British 4th Army led the attack, supported by ten Allied divisions, including troops from the colonies and the US. The British preliminary forces were able to deal a significant blow to the German line, and their strike was followed by tank reinforcements.

The element of surprise played a pivotal part in the Allies' success, who had switched from trying to soften the enemy's defenses with long artillery barrages to quick, concentrated attacks. In a single day, they managed to inflict about thirty thousand casualties on the Germans, who were forced to retreat, caught off-guard by the Allied attack. By the end of the battle, the Allies had gained significant ground, pushing into the German positions south of the Somme.

The events at Amiens were quickly followed by the Battle of Albert on August 21st, which was initiated by the British 3rd Army. Although smaller in scale, the Allied efforts were nevertheless successful, creating another gap in the German positions, which was swiftly exploited by the newly victorious 4th Army. The soldiers swept in from the flank and routed the Germans, who were again forced to retreat.

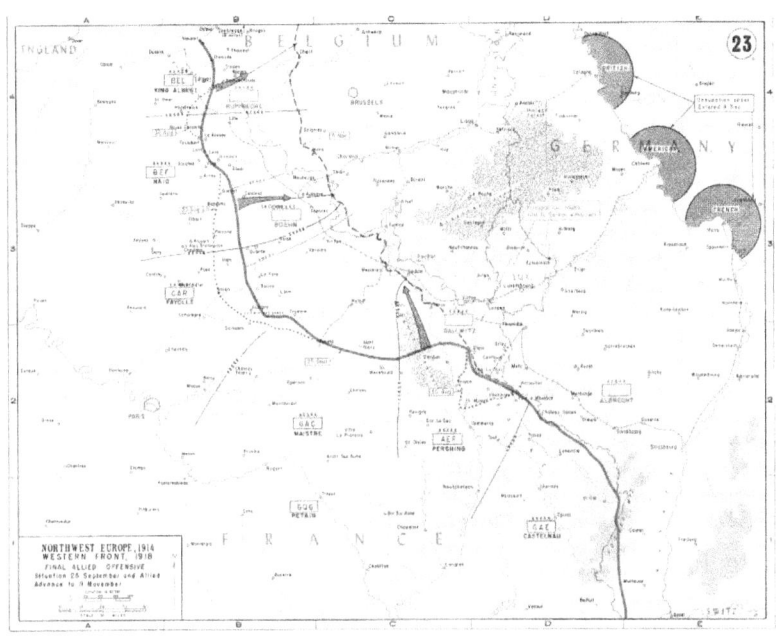

The Hundred Days Offensive.
https://commons.wikimedia.org/wiki/File:Western_front_1918_allied.jpg

Following these advances and the unrelenting pressure of the Allies on their positions, the German high command seemed, for the first time, pessimistic about continuing the war effort. On September 2nd, General Ludendorff ordered all the German forces to fall back to the Hindenburg Line, giving up any headway the Germans had made during the Spring Offensive. In fact, Ludendorff was one of the first to recognize the impending doom of the German army and tried to urge the Kaiser to engage in peace negotiations. With nearly 100,000 soldiers taken prisoner since the start of the Allied offensive, Ludendorff consulted with other high-ranking German officials, as well as the Austro-Hungarian high command, on the state of the war. Perhaps it was too late, as the responses from both were increasingly gloomy. Austria-Hungary even responded by saying they could only afford to continue fighting by the end of November. The pessimism showed after about two weeks when Emperor Charles I of Austria tried sending a letter to the Allies to express his wish to negotiate peace to avoid a total catastrophe. A day later, the Germans also followed through, offering a separate peace agreement to Belgium. However, the Allies realized their comfortable position and their advantageous position in the war and declined both offers.

What followed was the total annihilation of the remaining German troops by the Allied forces on the Western Front. The confidence level of the Allies reached an all-time high, with thousands of American reinforcements arriving every day in France and being transported right to the front lines. On top of that, Germany had tried to sue for peace. Every positive thing mounted up and gave a huge morale boost to the Allied soldiers. The Allies did not take their foot off the gas pedal after their victories at Amiens and Albert, exerting continuous pressure on the Germans and never stopping their attacks. The British forces achieved multiple breakthroughs with the Battle of Mont Saint-Quentin on August 31st, while the French and American soldiers converged on the Hindenburg Line in the south.

Aiming to cut off German supply lines and communication, the French and the AEF initiated the Meuse-Argonne Offensive on September 26th. At the same time, King Albert I of Belgium commanded a united Belgian, British, and French army at the Battle of Ypres in Flanders, seeking to break through at two different positions. Both attacks were successful, with the Allies exploiting their numerical superiority and overwhelming the German positions. After securing the northern and southern flanks, the Allies then converged on the central stretch of the

Hindenburg Line. Recognizing their advantage, the British 4th Army and the French 1st Army engaged at St. Quentin on September 29th and crushed the Germans, who were forced to retreat and abandon much of their equipment. On October 8th, the victory at St. Quentin was followed by yet another victory at Cambrai by the 1st and 3rd British Armies, which was the final straw. The Hindenburg Line had been overwhelmed, and the German mainland was exposed.

Victory in the Balkans

In addition to achieving success on the Western Front and the Middle East, the Allies were also able to finally break through against the Bulgarian defenses in the Balkan theater. The stalemate that had ensued after the events of the Salonica offensive had brought the conflict in the Balkans to an almost complete standstill, something that resembled the stalemate on the Western Front in 1915. The Central Powers did not wish to advance since they did not have any valuable objectives to take in the Balkans after the fall of Serbia, despite the fact that Greece entered the war on the side of the Allies in mid-1917. In addition, the Central Powers lacked resources and preferred to transfer troops after Serbia's defeat to other conflict zones, especially to Romania, whose short-lived participation actually held up a sizeable Central Powers' army for months.

After months of inactivity and small-scale fighting, the Allied troops decided to launch an offensive in September 1918, perhaps motivated by their success in other theaters. The Vardar Offensive, which was launched on September 15th, mainly envisioned overwhelming the Bulgarian trenches in Macedonia. The Allies had correctly recognized that the Bulgarians had exhausted their resources after years of prolonged fighting and believed that a breakthrough would be decisive enough to force the complete collapse of the Bulgarian forces.

From the beginning of the attacks, it was evident that the Allies would emerge victorious, as their artillery bombardments significantly softened up the Bulgarian defenses in the trenches, resulting in a relatively easy Allied victory at Dobro Pole. Two days later, another Allied force, consisting of French, British, Serbian, Greek, and Italian troops under the command of French General Louis d'Espèrey, achieved another victory near Lake Doiran, which shattered the Bulgarians' morale and forced them to retreat. However, unlike other instances when the Allies were reluctant to push their advantage right after achieving victories, d'Espèrey ordered his troops to chase down the fleeing Bulgarians, something that proved to be extremely effective. Although the Allied advance was stretched somewhat thin by September 20th, the Bulgarians had virtually nothing to answer them with.

The word of the defeat spread quickly in Bulgaria, as well as to the rest of the Central Powers. Since all of the Allied advances were largely simultaneous, it resulted in a massive domino effect. The Ottoman Empire, for example, had suffered defeats in the Middle East and was increasingly wary of Allied advances in the Balkans, which threatened the safety of Istanbul. Bulgaria was swept up in a nationwide protest, resulting in the Radomir Rebellion, which blamed the monarchy for the recent defeats. By September 29th, the Allies had made even more progress, taking Skopje and threatening to encircle and capture the remaining Bulgarian forces.

On the same day, the Bulgarian delegation, having already deemed the continuation of the war impossible, arrived in Salonica to meet with the Allies and sign an armistice. It was yet another defeat for the Central Powers, which now had their southern flank and the heart of Austria-Hungary's territories exposed to the Allies. The instability and rebellion in Bulgaria forced Tsar Ferdinand I to abdicate and go into exile. Meanwhile, the Allies split up their forces to close in on Budapest and Istanbul.

Chapter Fifteen – The War Ends

With the Ottoman Empire and Bulgaria forced to sign separate armistices with the Allies, the rest of the Central Powers—Germany and Austria-Hungary—knew their days were numbered. The Allies had also overwhelmed the German defenses at the Hindenburg Line and threatened to advance through the heart of Germany, while Austro-Hungarian clashes on the Italian front had produced a disastrous stalemate and demoralized the Austro-Hungarian soldiers. Faced with crisis after crisis, the Central Powers realized they had lost the war.

The Final Surrender

By October of 1918, all of Germany knew that the war had been lost. There was no possible way in which the Central Powers could recover from their losses. The German high command felt humiliated, as they could not effectively end the war in their favor, despite the initial success they had seen in the first two years of the war. In a desperate move, the German naval command ordered the High Seas Fleet to engage in a final decisive battle against the British Royal Navy, which had choked out the former in the North Sea and had clearly asserted its dominance over the seas throughout the course of the war.

However, after receiving these orders in late October, the German sailors refused to leave the ports to fight, believing that the battle would have no value since the war was already lost. The word of the mutinies of Wilhelmshaven and Kiel on October 29th and November 3rd quickly spread throughout the desperate, war-torn country. Eventually, it amounted to something much bigger than soldiers disregarding orders.

Participants of the sailor's revolt took to the streets, inciting similar anti-war protests throughout Germany. In Berlin, thousands of people protested the war, believing that their lives had been negatively affected by years of conflict. Things were not looking great for the monarchy and the government, which decided to proceed somewhat peacefully by not trying to violently crush the revolts. On November 9th, 1918, the protesters, led by the leaders of the German Social Democratic Party, proclaimed a republic instead of the imperial monarchy, forcing Kaiser Wilhelm II to flee the country and abdicate in the coming weeks. Prince Maximillian von Baden, the chancellor who had been appointed in early October, ceded his office to Friedrich Ebert. The revolutionaries had triumphed.

Protesters in Germany during the revolution.
https://commons.wikimedia.org/wiki/File:Germany_at_the_End_of_the_First_World_Wa r,_Including_Scenes_of_the_German_Revolution,_1918-1919._MH34191.jpg

The new government's first move was to sue for peace. The negotiations of a potential armistice and peace terms were already being discussed in October in Germany and among the Allies, who were confident they had won. Two days after the revolution's success, the German delegation, led by Matthias Erzberger, arrived at the front lines and met with the Allied high command. The two sides started to discuss terms, although the Germans had nothing to negotiate with. The German high command had made it clear to accept all terms of the armistice to immediately stop the fighting and avoid any more casualties. On November 11th, the Germans accepted the terms of the armistice presented. It was a humiliating display, as the Germans were forced to demobilize their army, surrender all of their military equipment and guns, and evacuate their forces from all locations. Germany was out of the war. It had been defeated and torn apart, but it still had to await the final consequences.

Parallel to the events of the revolution, a separate armistice was signed by Austria-Hungary on November 3rd with the Italians. After months of stalemate, the decisive battle that decided the fate of the war was the Battle of Vittorio Veneto, where the Italians, supported by other Allied divisions, finally achieved a significant victory, inflicting more than 500,000 casualties on the Austro-Hungarians. This marked the end of fighting on the Italian front.

The Austro-Hungarians, much like their German allies, had exhausted all of their resources, and the toll of the war had been evident on the population. Pietro Badoglio and an Austro-Hungarian delegation led by General Viktor von Webenau signed the armistice at Villa Giusti, which was outside of the small town of Padua in northeastern Italy. The armistice was put into effect the very next day. Austria-Hungary was forced to retreat back to the pre-war borders and evacuate all of its troops. Italy moved in to occupy Innsbruck and North Tyrol with about twenty thousand men.

The Paris Peace Conference

With the separate armistices signed by all four of the Central Powers, the war was finally over. The fighting stopped in November on all fronts, and soldiers from both sides abandoned their positions. As the defeated countries started carrying out the terms of the different armistices, the Allied nations rejoiced. For France and Britain, the successful end of the war brought a much-needed sigh of relief. After millions dead, different towns and settlements destroyed, and the landscape torn apart from years of heavy artillery fire, the Allies expected their victory to have been worth it. Thus, in order to formally end the war, the victorious nations organized a conference in Paris to start peace negotiations with the defeated countries and decide what was next for the world, which had just experienced the bloodiest conflict in history so far.

In the ensuing Paris Peace Conference, which started in January 1919, representatives from thirty-two nations around the world assembled to create a new world order, something that was very much reminiscent of the Congress of Vienna after the defeat of Napoleon. Although the formal peace negotiations would last until 1923, the outcome of the talks was based on the Paris Peace Conference.

The beginning of the conference was stalled until January, mostly by British Prime Minister David Lloyd George, who wanted to wait for the results of domestic elections before engaging in negotiations. The "Big Four" presided over the negotiations and had largely agreed upon the outcome by privately consulting with each other. The "Big Four" consisted of Britain, represented by a delegation led by Prime Minister David Lloyd George; President Woodrow Wilson of the US, whose unfortunate illness caused Robert Lansing to assume his position; Prime Minister Georges Clemenceau of France; and Italian Prime Minister Vittorio Emanuele Orlando. Japan, the other major Allied power, is often excluded from the "Big Four" by historians, despite the fact that it was well represented during the conference and achieved favorable gains from the talks.

Representatives also assembled from the British Dominion, including Canada, Australia, India, South Africa, and New Zealand, although they were regarded as "supporters" of British views and assigned the status of minor powers due to their heavy contribution to the overall war effort. Delegations were present from the remaining belligerents of the war, like Greece and Romania, while the Serbs were represented together with the Croats and Slovenes. In addition to those nations, delegations were present from South and Central America, as well as from Asia. Finally, some delegations represented countries that sought international recognition and sovereignty, such as the Baltic states, Ukraine, the Caucasus, and so on. All in all, the Paris Peace Conference included nearly all of the existing sovereign countries in the world, something that stressed the importance of the conference even more.

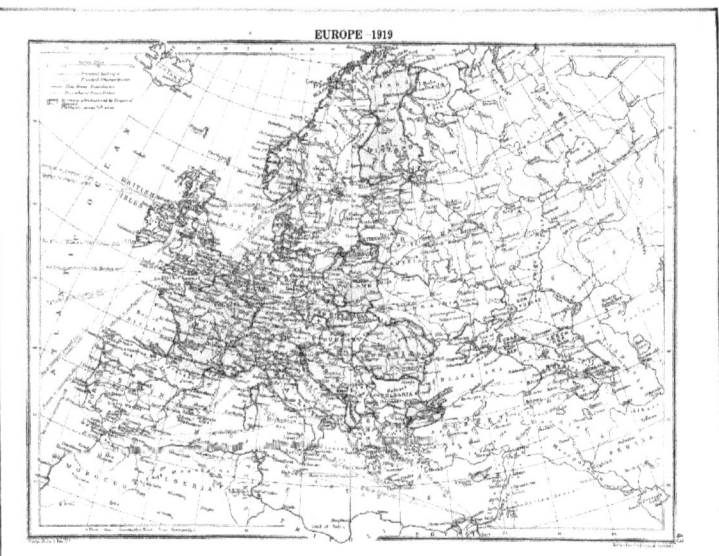

Europe after the Paris Peace Conference.

https://commons.wikimedia.org/wiki/File:Europe_map_1919.jpg

As expected, the negotiations were led by the victorious nations, which sought to maximize their gains while also weakening the defeated belligerents as much as possible to avoid another war from breaking out on the same scale and magnitude. The five official peace treaties that would be signed by the Allies and members of the Central Powers were prepared over the course of the conference. These included the infamous Treaty of Versailles with Germany, signed on June 28th, 1919; the Treaties of Saint-Germain and Trianon, which were signed separately by the two monarchies of Austria and Hungary on September 10th, 1919, and June 4th, 1920, respectively; the Treaty of Neuilly with Bulgaria, signed on November 27th, 1919; and, finally, the Treaty of Sèvres with the Ottoman Empire on August 10th, 1920, which would be replaced by the Treaty of Lausanne three years later.

In addition to these treaties, an important outcome of the Paris Peace Conference was the formation of the League of Nations, the first international organization that sought to establish and preserve world peace. The creation of the League of Nations was largely influenced by President Woodrow Wilson in his efforts to spread what is now referred to as "Wilsonian idealism," an approach to international relations that endorses demilitarization, cooperation, and a peaceful resolution. President Wilson had propagated the idea of international cooperation since his famous "Fourteen Points" speech in January 1918, where he proposed the fourteen terms that should be reached for an effective conclusion of World War I. Throughout the Paris Peace Conference, America's decisions were largely shaped by this concept, which envisioned the creation of a peaceful international community and the pursuit of a united plan of action, one based on mutual friendship rather than rivalry.

Aftermath

The Paris Peace Conference had an immense impact on the world, as it decided the lives of millions of people. The Allies, finally having achieved victory after four years of brutal fighting and experiencing hardship after hardship, made sure to leverage their privilege as the victors. Out of the five treaties that were agreed upon in the conference, the Treaty of Versailles was undoubtedly the harshest and had massive implications for decades to come. It was signed in the Palace of Versailles almost fifty years after the formal creation of the German Empire.

The Allies made Germany suffer the most out of the defeated nations. According to the humiliating terms of the agreement, Germany agreed to take all the blame for causing World War I and the subsequent damage and loss of life that had transpired during the conflict. It clearly outlined Germany as the main aggressor in the war. The Allies also made Germany sign off on the complete demobilization and dissolution of its army. In addition, Germany had to make substantial territorial concessions, giving up about 10 percent of its European territories and all of its overseas colonies, which were swiftly divided between Britain, France, and Japan. Germany was also forced to pay an absurd amount in war reparations for the damages it had caused to the Allied nations. the total amounted to about 132 billion German marks, which is equivalent to about 270 billion USD today.

All of these measures were taken to make sure that Germany would never rise up again and contest the Great Powers' superiority on the continent. The French were exceptionally hard on the Germans, as they had a personal score to settle with the Germans. They took back control of the Alsace and Lorraine provinces they had lost in 1871.

All in all, the Treaty of Versailles had a devastating effect on Germany. The economy was in ruins after the war, and massive international and domestic debt meant there was little room to improve the situation. The newly established

Weimar Republic—a name temporarily adopted by Germany after the revolution—had no way of dealing with the problems that cropped up after the Paris Peace Conference. Germany's international role was reduced beyond belief, and to ensure that Germany stayed pacified, the Allies occupied the Rhineland for the next fifteen years, with troops present at all times.

The German public had lost all hope of retaliation and was faced with extreme poverty, hunger, and tough living conditions. This, in turn, incited a sense of hatred toward the Allies, something that would finally be exploited in the 1930s by the Nazi Party and the rise of Hitler. Germany's humiliation made it possible for radical nationalist movements to become prominent in the country as time passed by, with more and more people being upset over the fact that the whole war had been blamed on them by their enemies. It would have been interesting to see how Germany would have developed if the international community had actually helped Germany recover instead of overly punishing it after the war.

The German Empire was not the only one that saw disastrous outcomes after the war. Austria-Hungary, as a single political entity, was disbanded, and in the lands previously controlled by the dual monarchy, new democratic nation-states were established. Some parts were absorbed by Italy, as promised by the Allies. With Austria-Hungary's dissolution, the political landscape of Europe was completely altered, and a new power dynamic emerged. All of those nations that had previously been under the control of the Habsburgs finally achieved freedom, and their sovereignty was internationally recognized, giving these young states new hopes and aspirations to pursue. Among the newly formed nations were Poland (for the first time in over a century), Ukraine, Belarus, Czechoslovakia, the separate states of Austria and Hungary, as well as a new Yugoslavian state, which had been predominantly inhabited by Serbs, Croats, and Slovenes.

It was also an end for the Ottoman Empire, which was reduced to only its Anatolian territories, as well as the small European part of Constantinople (Istanbul). It lost all of its Middle Eastern and Mesopotamian territories, with France and Britain seizing control of the region and dividing it between themselves. There, the two European powers organized "protectorates," two separate spheres of influence, something which, in hindsight, further contributed to the rising tensions in the region during the rest of the 20th century. The Ottoman Empire was formally reestablished as the Republic of Turkey following the Paris Peace Conference.

This was the political landscape that emerged from the ashes of World War I. It completely changed Europe, with four fewer empires than there had been in 1914: the German Empire was now the Weimer Republic; Austria-Hungary had been divided into multiple smaller nations, including the separate republics of Austria and Hungary; Turkey replaced the Ottoman Empire; and, finally, the Russian Revolution of 1917 had seen the Russian Empire reorganized as a soviet state. A new world order was established, with clearly defined, internationally recognized state boundaries that were, in most cases, in line with the national boundaries of different peoples. Nationalism and liberty had triumphed, an outcome that seemed inevitable even before the start of the war.

Conclusion

The League of Nations was supposed to lead the new world into a period of peace and prosperity. While the mission of this first intergovernmental organization was noble and respectable, as time would show, it would not be able to achieve its goals. The League of Nations could not hold a firm grip over the actions of sovereign nations, which were still motivated by self-interest and pursued their national goals instead of what was best for the international community. Other members of the League of Nations watched these states from a distance, reluctant to intervene on multiple occasions and reassert the organization's dominance. Thus, over time, the League of Nations lost its role and importance. A peaceful and prosperous world, one built on cooperation and mutual understanding as perceived by President Wilson, was challenged by individual actors that destroyed the organization's credibility. The inability of the League of Nations to act eventually manifested itself in World War II, which broke out just twenty-one years after the end of World War I.

The Great War had brought destruction on a previously unseen scale, with an estimated forty million casualties on both sides. About ten million civilians around the world were lost, in addition to about the same number of military personnel. While it is difficult to know the exact number of people whose lives were affected by the war, it is clear when observing the post-war states of the belligerents that the effects of the war lasted for years. Those soldiers who survived relentless, non-stop fighting on the front lines suffered from severe anxiety, PTSD, and other psychological problems. Living in such harsh conditions for months on end, under the threat of constant shelling by enemy artillery and in muddy, overcrowded trenches with low supplies, had certainly taken its toll on the survivors. As they returned back from the war to their homes, they had to pass through miles of destroyed terrain and hundreds of ruined towns.

In the end, the First World War only became "the First" after the events of the 1940s, which saw the world plunge into turmoil again, although the Second World War was far more catastrophic. The First World War did not "stop all conflicts," as many had predicted, including the winners. What emerged from the ruins was a more complex global system, in which the war's winners enjoyed various privileges while the losers were purposefully isolated and made to feel guilty for the world's problems.

The victorious nations attempted to enact policies that would maintain peace and stability throughout the period of recovery, but their efforts were in vain, as the international order formed immediately after World War I would only continue for thirty years. Their efforts failed terribly, and the world's rapid collapse into yet another world war in 1939 made everyone recognize that the paradigm adopted after 1918 was fundamentally flawed. It had been based on the redistribution of power at the expense of millions of people living in the defeated nations. The losers' suffering was effectively exploited by the winners, but no one anticipated that their efforts would result in another conflict that would eclipse the First World War in nearly every way.

Here's another book by Enthralling History that you might like

Free limited time bonus

Stop for a moment. We have a free bonus set up for you. The problem is this: we forget 90% of everything that we read after 7 days. Crazy fact, right? Here's the solution: we've created a printable, 1-page pdf summary for this book that you're reading now. All you have to do to get your free pdf summary is to go to the following website: **https://livetolearn.lpages.co/enthrallinghistory/**

Once you do, it will be intuitive. Enjoy, and thank you!

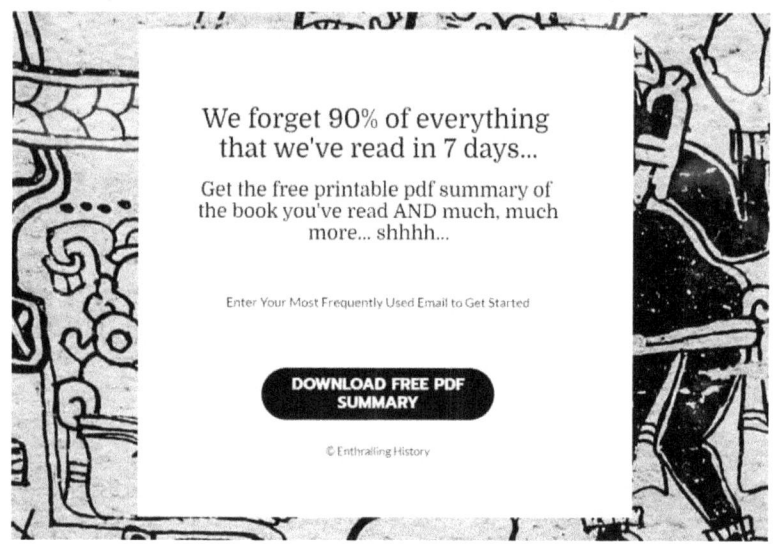

Sources

- Mann, Tara. World War I, edited by Jacob Steinberg, Rosen Publishing Group, 2016. ProQuest eBook Central, *https://ebookcentral.proquest.com/lib/jacob/detail.action?docID=4573489.*
- Rajczak, Nelson, Kristen. World War I, Cavendish Square Publishing LLC, 2021. ProQuest eBook Central, *https://ebookcentral.proquest.com/lib/jacob/detail.action?docID=6710737.*
- Gagne, Tammy. World War I Technology, ABDO Publishing Company, 2017. ProQuest eBook Central, *https://ebookcentral.proquest.com/lib/jacob/detail.action?docID=5263040.*
- 50MINUTES. World War I: Part Two: 1915-1917: Stalemate, Lemaitre Publishing, 2017. ProQuest eBook Central, *https://ebookcentral.proquest.com/lib/jacob/detail.action?docID=4815644.*
- Williamson, Samuel R. "The Origins of World War I." The Journal of Interdisciplinary History, vol. 18, no. 4, 1988, pp. 795-818. JSTOR, *https://doi.org/10.2307/204825*
- Van Evera, Stephen. "The Cult of the Offensive and the Origins of the First World War." International Security, vol. 9, no. 1, 1984, pp. 58-107. JSTOR, *https://doi.org/10.2307/2538636*
- Kaiser, David E. "Germany and the Origins of the First World War." The Journal of Modern History, vol. 55, no. 3, 1983, pp. 442-74. JSTOR, *http://www.jstor.org/stable/1878597*

- Gompert, David C., et al. "Woodrow Wilson's Decision to Enter World War I, 1917." Blinders, Blunders, and Wars: What America and China Can Learn, RAND Corporation, 2014, pp. 71-80. JSTOR, *http://www.jstor.org/stable/10.7249/j.ctt1287m9t.13*
- Crook, Paul, and David Paul Crook. Darwinism, War and History: The Debate over the Biology of War from the "Origin of Species" to the First World War. Cambridge University Press, 1994.
- Hart, BH Liddell. A History of the First World War. Pan Macmillan, 2014.
- Horne, John. "The Global Legacies of World War I." Current History, vol. 113, no. 766, 2014, pp. 299-304. JSTOR, *http://www.jstor.org/stable/45388568*
- Chamberlin, William Henry. "The First Russian Revolution." The Russian Review, vol. 26, no. 1, 1967, pp. 4-12. JSTOR, *https://doi.org/10.2307/126860*
- Wade, Rex A. The Russian Revolution, 1917. Vol. 53. Cambridge University Press, 2017.
- Yeh, Puong Fei. "The Role of the Zimmermann Telegram in Spurring America's Entry into the First World War." American Intelligence Journal 32.1 (2015): 61-64.
- Schindler, John. "Steamrollered in Galicia: The Austro-Hungarian Army and the Brusilov Offensive, 1916." War in History, vol. 10, no. 1, 2003, pp. 27-59. JSTOR, *http://www.jstor.org/stable/26061940*
- John A. C. Conybeare, and Todd Sandler. "The Triple Entente and the Triple Alliance 1880-1914: A Collective Goods Approach." The American Political Science Review, vol. 84, no. 4, 1990, pp. 1197-206. JSTOR, *https://doi.org/10.2307/1963259*
- Morgan, Elizabeth, and Robert Green. World War I and the Rise of Global Conflict, Greenhaven Publishing LLC, 2016. ProQuest eBook Central, *https://ebookcentral.proquest.com/lib/jacob/detail.action?docID=5538452*
- Baldwin, Faith, and Stig Förster. The Treaty of Versailles: A Reassessment after 75 Years. Cambridge University Press, 1998.
- Lu, Catherine. "Justice and Moral Regeneration: Lessons from the Treaty of Versailles." International Studies Review, vol. 4, no. 3, 2002, pp. 3-25. JSTOR, *http://www.jstor.org/stable/3186461*

www.ingramcontent.com/pod-product-compliance
Lightning Source LLC
Chambersburg PA
CBHW070327010526
44107CB00004B/447